FINITE LADDERS

FINITE LADDERS

The Elements of Creative Thinking

Trevor Swadling

First published in Australia
First edition 2023

Copyright © Trevor Swadling 2022
All rights reserved.
The moral right of the author has been asserted.
trevorswadling@gmail.com

Trade Paperback ISBN: 978-0-646-87442-5
Hardcover ISBN: 978-0-6457954-9-3
E. Book ISBN: 978-0-6547954-8-6
Book cover and formatting: Design Direction – Verner Verass

*This book is dedicated to my wife, Kathleen
for her love and support as well as
her tireless editing and input.*

CONTENTS

PREFACE 1
INTRODUCTION 5

CHAPTER 1

FINDING THE COMPONENTS OF THINKING 7
Let's Think About Our Thinking 7
Enlarging Our Circumscribed View 13
Exploring Our Reality 14

CHAPTER 2

DISCOVERING THE ELEMENTS OF
REFLECTIVE THINKING 19
Emerging Science, New Philosophies, & Transition 21
Scientific Method and Postmodernism 27

CHAPTER 3

THE EMERGING RELATIONAL ELEMENTS—OUR
VALUE SYSTEM 37
Finding the Keystone—the Value Driver of Choice 43

CHAPTER 4

OUR QUEST FOR THE HIGHEST VALUE 53
Love Is an Empty Vessel Unless Shared 56

CHAPTER 5

EMBRACING THE CORE OF SPIRIT REALITIES.................... 61
Spring Has Emerged and Life is Astir 63
Differing Lenses of Perception 66
One Might Ask the Question.. 71
Where is God?.. 74
Brain Capacity & the "God Spot"..................................... 76
Objective & Subjective Time... 80

CHAPTER 6

LOCATING THE ORIGIN OF LOVE—A FAMILY AFFAIR........ 83
The Enlarged Family—A Universe Affair........................... 89

CHAPTER 7

PERSONALITY, CONSCIENCE, & SPIRIT REALITIES............. 97
An Attempt to Define Personality 97
The Confusion Surrounding Conscience.......................... 101
Spirit-Value Realities... 103
It's Not Just All About Matter and Energy....................... 105

CHAPTER 8

NATURAL BLOCKERS TO THE GOODNESS OF LOVE.......... 109
Why Do Civilisations Fall?.. 112

CHAPTER 9

TRANSFERRING OUR SEAT OF IDENTITY........................ 115
Where Does the Soul Fit into the Picture?...................... 117

CHAPTER 10

THE WOMB OF FINITE REALITY & OUR BIRTH 121

CHAPTER 11

RELIGION AND SOCIETY 127
Social Cohesion—a Collective Consciousness 130
Finding the Compass.. 137
A Lasting and Cohesive Nucleus for Humanity 140

CHAPTER 12

RENEWING OUR KEYSTONE 147
Positional Values 149

CONCLUSION 159

REFERENCES 162

PREFACE

This is a book about trying to work it out; an appraisal if you like of how we process and understand reality. It is an investigation into the thinking processes of our minds and an attempt to discover how our minds innately work and grow. By understanding how our minds interact with, and process reality, our self-awareness can increase and put us in a better position for greater self-control in directing our life journey.

I've tried to base this work on observable facts, so for me—and I hope for you—it will not be a flight into unreasonable speculation, nor one that dives too deeply into the depths of the metaphysical. I'm hoping this book will serve as a practical guide that fleshes out an understanding of the tools we use in the "hands on" workings of our minds as we go forth in accumulating and utilising our experiences.

I must say that I have found the majority of people I've befriended, and had conversations with over the years, are interested in talking about how their minds work; they are also interested in truth no matter what level of education or walk of life, country, or culture they come from. Many people realise early on in their lives that it's better to suffer the consequences of truth than to tell a lie e.g., young children, because they are intelligent, sometimes tend towards telling lies to avoid being caught out, especially if they find they can get away with it. But as we grow within our social environment an awareness of our developing moral conscience may dictate that it is better to follow what we consciously know to be true. If we choose to follow what we know to be right we're more likely to gain the ability to strengthen and clarify our foundation and reference for our framework for thinking. This process is basic and is an important part of growing up.

Each time we sincerely pursue and embrace our understanding of truth, upon reflection we can realise that this is how we grow and mature. Over time we can acquire experience-based wisdom simply through the pursuit of truth. Wisdom acquired through honesty and personal experience is a worthy goal for personal attainment.

I've observed and realised that most of us are not scoundrels; we're sometimes forgetful and oftentimes weak because we're only human. We're incomplete and not highly conscious of the innate functioning of our minds and thinking processes. We don't naturally think a great deal about our thinking. We don't always give ourselves enough time to think things through thoroughly. We are a work in progress—a wonderful beginning of possibilities and potentials; we are a growing and emerging personal reality. For these reasons we should make the effort to become respectful of others and attempt to be aware of their individual circumstances with an understanding that we are all struggling with the same kinds of challenges due to our incompleteness, even though we are full of amazing potentials. Sometimes we can set off a spark in others to be interested in truth. We should never be afraid to share our experiences and ideas and even thoughts about our values.

"Children are permanently impressed only by the loyalties of their adult associates; precept or even example is not lastingly influential. Loyal persons are growing persons, and growth is an impressive and inspiring reality. Live loyally today — grow — and tomorrow will attend to itself. The quickest way for a tadpole to become a frog is to live loyally each moment as a tadpole." [2]

INTRODUCTION

Mind is our interface between us and reality. By observing and identifying the various components that drive our thinking processes and influence our motivations and choices, we can get a better understanding of why we do what we do. By exploring how our minds naturally work I believe we can position ourselves to develop greater opportunities and potentials for gaining increased clarity and creativity as we grow.

Holistic reality is made up of just three basic elements which we will be identifying as the basic tools that our minds use to develop a construct that also includes additional related elements of reality that emerge through our experiences. By understanding the emerging elements, we will find that they are essential tools to guide us in our thinking processes that will add greater depth of perspective to our understanding and perception of the wholeness of reality.

I'm going to propose and outline a new way of thinking—to suggest a new framework in which we can think that has fundamental tools that are understandable, relevant and common to us all. It's not complex but is one which can assist us in building and strengthening our intuition, insight, and creativity. As our minds grow and develop in comprehending reality, we can use our minds as "finite ladders" to climb and to see a little further and attempt to make our "selves"—

our personalities—more unified and real.

So, the idea developed in the following chapters explores how we can expand our conscious mind to view reality from broader perspectives so we can function with a greater capacity of awareness. We'll be doing this by first exploring how our mind works with the basic elements of reality. We will then investigate how other relational elements of reality *emerge* through our experiences with the first set of basic elements. After that we will finally look at the combination of all these elements when blended together; we will discover that they create new value frameworks in which to think.

The universe we live in is a wonderful and mysterious place, and our minds are innately equipped to embark on an alluring adventure of discovery. The mind can be likened to a living instrument on which each person can choose to play the uplifting melodies of relational harmonics. We are the personal creative composers and players of our minds. Music is inherently based on mathematics and the basic elements of music are just seven tones and five semi-tones. These twelve notes can be arranged and rearranged in a myriad of ways to form cord structures and scales that we can apply in an almost infinite variety of combinations to produce music. With practice and the acquirement of skill, along with an understanding of the basic mathematics of music, musicians can bring forth exquisite melodies. As with our minds, to avoid playing the wrong notes and producing discord instead of harmony it helps to have a basic understanding of how the mind works with reality and identify the emerging relational elements that go towards the quality of its make up. We each have the potential and responsibility within us to contribute to the creation of finite reality as we are all incredibly unique and can be of tremendous value to one another. Collectively we can—over time—make a truly good and beautiful finite world for our children to build upon for future generations that follow.

CHAPTER 1

Finding the Components of Thinking

Let's Think About Our Thinking

Before we delve too deeply into this topic, it's important to be mindful that our understanding of the totality of reality within and around us is limited because our understanding and insights go hand-in-hand with our time and experience. Our resource libraries of knowledge that we draw on for thinking will be constantly evolving and growing; there will always be room for ongoing revision and improvement. A genuine sincerity will be an important factor for growth. So, with this in the back of our minds, let's think about thinking.

We begin by looking out—observing—then we usually react before we reflect and fully process the realisation of the consequences of our reactions. In other words, we don't always "look before we leap." We perceive the world and the universe from our individual perspectives hence we are the driver; we are in charge; the mind is simply relaying the information we need in order to make a decision. To develop good habits of thinking it is important to understand the basic elements that our mind naturally uses. Once we realise the innate decision-making processes regarding these elements, we should be in a better position to have more control in making intelligent and well-considered decisions.

"We cannot solve our problems with the same thinking we used when we created them." – *Albert Einstein* [1]

With this understanding in mind, we need to discover the very basis for intelligent rational thought because we are attempting to build upon this foundation a growing, living structure in which we think, live, act, and have our being. So it would help to understand what the building blocks—or basic elements—are that will make up the foundation of our thinking because we need to have a strong, stable, and reliable foundational footing to carry the load.

So, what are these basic elements of reality that we need to understand and consider so that we may appreciate the wholeness of their relationship with one another? For now, I'll refer to them as **things, meanings, and values.** By pausing to consider these three elements of our thinking we can better evaluate the outcomes of our actions, for as Albert Einstein so aptly said: "Education is not the learning of facts, it's rather the training of the mind to think." (I'll be elaborating on the basic elements of reality a little later.)

There are so many variables of life to consider, many with not so happy outcomes when played out. The sea of humanity is littered with misunderstandings, dead-ends, carnage, and disaster. But contained alongside these mishaps and human foibles are the ongoing evolving successes. Even by making mistakes and suffering the consequences we learn and acquire wisdom—nothing of value is lost. The good that can come out of our mistakes can outweigh the bad and give us the upper hand as we keep an eye on the future. As we move forward let's always remember that in the creative landscape of life, it is the black spots that appear so ugly because they simply stand out against a white background. There is and will always be more goodness in the creativity of life within our world.

CHAPTER 1

"The important thing is not to stop questioning. Curiosity has its own reason for existing." – *Albert Einstein* [1]

The universe is mysterious; there is so much about it that we are yet to discover, observe, and discern. The same can be said about us and our inner-selves, and what makes up our seat of identity. Do we reside in the brain or in the mind? Is the physical brain literally the mind or is the mind something separate from the brain but interfaces and functions within the brain? What is there about our "selves" that we haven't yet fully understood? What are all the components that contribute to our "identity" and what constitutes our thinking process?

There is ongoing research being done on how our brains and our inner lives work. The findings produce a plethora of facts, theories, and questions that stimulate ongoing postulation and discussion. Science may never be able to prove or provide definite answers to the origins of life and mind but nevertheless, here is an interesting quote to contemplate the ongoing search for answers to **their origins:**

"The source of the streams of universe life and of the cosmic mind must be above the levels of their manifestation. The human mind cannot be consistently explained in terms of the lower orders of existence." [2]

Before we move on, I would like to share with you some extracts from three interesting threads of discussion that have different points of view about the definition of mind and brain from Research Gate, which is one of the many discussion blogs on the Web about the brain and mind:

Opinion 1: "From my strict materialist perspective (which, of course, could ultimately be wrong in the end), questions such as "What is the mind?" or "Where is the mind?" are ultimately meaningless questions. A brain asking these kinds of questions is somewhat analogous to a finger trying to point at its own tip; in my view, the mind is merely an illusion created by one's neural network responding to its own activity. A feedback loop, if you will. ... If one wishes to assume that there is a specific location in the brain or body where this neuronal activity is monitored, or where this feedback loop resides, then one is merely talking about the location where "consciousness" is seated. And questions about what creates or, determines consciousness are, I think, the fascinating, relevant, and important ones we are facing now." [3]

Opinion 2: "Dualism is the concept that our mind is more than just our brain. This concept entails that our mind has a non-material, spiritual dimension that includes consciousness and possibly an eternal attribute. One way to understand this concept is to consider our self as a container including our physical body and physical brain along with a separate non-physical mind, spirit, or soul. The mind, spirit, or soul is considered the conscious part that manifests itself through the brain in a similar way that picture waves and sound waves manifest themselves through a television set. The picture and sound waves are also non-material just like the mind, spirit, or soul.

"The alternative concept is materialism. Materialism holds that everything in our universe is made from physical materials including the human mind or brain and that spiritual attributes do not exist in the universe. This concept holds that our mind and brain are one and the same.

"If dualism is not true, the mind is limited to the physical brain. Assuming this scenario, what kind of a mind would we expect? We certainly would not expect to have consciousness strictly from materials. Perhaps we could expect to see a mechanical mind similar to a computer that is run by a program. We would not expect things like consciousness, sensations, thoughts, emotions, desires, beliefs, and free choice. Such a mind would behave in a deterministic way based upon the laws of matter. Many scientists and philosophers are now concluding that the laws of chemistry and physics cannot explain the experience of consciousness in human beings.

"We would not expect people with such a mind to be responsible for their behaviour because everything they do is determined by the attributes of matter. We all know that is absurd. Also, we could not trust our minds since they are just a random collection of materials not produced by an intelligent mind." [3]

Opinion 3: "The brain is an organ but the mind isn't. The mind is the manifestations of thought, perception, emotion, determination, memory and imagination that take place within the brain. Mind is often used to refer especially to the thought processes of reason. The mind is the awareness of consciousness we know, the ability to control what we do, and know what we are doing and why. It is the ability to understand." [3]

This is a fascinating subject with differing points of view, but there is a consensus that mind gives us the ability to understand; it has memory and imagination and functions as a thought processor of reason. While there are different views on the origins of mind all agree that the experience of consciousness and its freewill remains a mystery.

Regardless of whether the brain exists alone or whether the mind in-circuits it, what we do know is that the brain is a living material electro-chemical organ that automatically looks after the many functions of our material life vehicle while at the same time functioning with, or as a mind. Most agree that the consciousness of humans is a big mystery just as the source of life and mind itself are. Regardless, we know our mind serves us well, and the important thing is that we can observe how it functions. I believe that the brain and mind are seamlessly interfaced and that our individual freewill is our **seat of identity** and freely uses the mind as a tool for creative thinking and action. Our personal life vehicle is made up of many different components; it is a growing living entity and when put together we function beautifully as one.

As civilization advances and as the world around us becomes more complex, there will be an ongoing need to understand the importance of consciously organising how we think and make decisions in the pursuit of truth. Our awareness needs to be expanded so our minds can serve us well in facing the multiple challenges of the future, therefore, we need to stay the course, and be honest and sincere with ourselves. To do this we need to find what it takes to achieve quality thinking and consistently apply it in problem solving.

As a species we are naturally curious, we have this adventurous spirit that can get us into a lot of trouble from time to time. Therefore, it's important for us to ponder and appreciate the beauty of simplicity first, because therein lie great truths that have the potential to stabilise our thinking. When we gain stability and direction in our thinking, we are better prepared to contemplate the complex.

Evolving reality starts out simply, and as it continues to evolve and grow it naturally becomes more complex. As civilizations and societies become more complex and specialised in their fields of endeavour, the more important and necessary it becomes for we as individuals to have a solid, reliable, and simple foundational framework for thinking; a framework where we have arranged and positioned our values where the focus of our value system successfully directs our creativity to take us where we want to go.

We need to ask ourselves questions such as, how do we want our world to be? How can we honestly discern where we actually are and decide where we want to go? How do we set worthy and attainable goals? Where do we place our relationship with others in our value system? How do we create unity of purpose while working towards our individual goals as well as our common goals with others? How do we move forward together in harmony in the pursuit of truth while maintaining our individuality? In the social arena we need to be sincere and fragrant, with an eye focused on living and working in harmony with one another.

"Life is really simple, but we insist on making it complicated."
– *Confucius* [4]

Enlarging Our Circumscribed View

We often take for granted many of our modern-day luxuries such as reading a book or working with an app on our electronic devices or having some quality time off for creative thinking. In the evening you might be sitting on a comfy couch reading an e-book and simply reach up and flick on the light with one finger. You might get up and go to the fridge to get yourself an icy cold drink. If you pause to consider how amazing it is that these things work so easily for us, you may realise just how far humans have come for us to have such luxuries at our fingertips. It's even a luxury to have the time to ponder these things and to just relax and read this! There is so much activity and industry behind the simple light switch. There are large mining companies with untold labourers and complex machinery;

there are train lines and shipping ports; factories for making things like electric cables, light bulbs, and switches; there are tree plantations supplying the lamp posts; substations and thousands of skilled workers such as installers, maintenance staff, power plant designers, and engineers who are all organised into teams to work and cooperate with one another. And that's just your light switch!

Primitive humans never had this luxury. They lived in a harsh environment which drove them to cooperate with each other for survival purposes! If I were a primitive man and sat down for too long getting lost in my thoughts, I could be stalked and torn to shreds by some wild beast or smacked over the head by someone in my clan for simply not pulling my weight. Life back then was pretty serious and intense; foraging for food and shelter, fighting off predators, defending your territory from other clans... not a lot of time to ponder or simply take the weekend off and relax in the sun. But all this harsh environment pushed humans forward. We had to organise ourselves; the hostile environment forced us to cooperate with one another and we gradually learnt the value of teamwork and leadership. We progressed and evolved our systems of self-maintenance and you and I now reap the benefits of a long history of the blood, sweat, and tears of past ages. It's a privilege to have all the conveniences and opportunities that we now enjoy!

"At first life was a struggle for existence; now, for a standard of living; next it will be for quality of thinking, the coming earthly goal of human existence." [2]

Exploring Our Reality

How do we perceive reality? Obviously, we perceive it through an innate process of the mind. Our mind just functions. Life switches it on, and it fills up and grows through experience in a natural and automatic way. Inside our mind we see a wonderful arena of choice in which our intent and freewill exists, thinks, decides and acts; it has a growing experiential memory-knowledge-interface between us and reality. We view the external world, then from within we process our experiences and formulate our reactions. It is the arena in which our thinking happens. The ultimate creative tool of mankind!

A person is more than a machine. If a person were just a machine, how did he or she come to the erroneous conclusion that they are a mere machine? A machine does not have the capacity to think that it is a machine. Humans are creative freewill personalities, capable of playing the notes to many emotional moods. Humans can play the discords of destruction or contribute to the uplifting melody and rhythm of participation in the adventure of discovering and contributing to the joys of life. The mathematical notes to all music in the universe are there for us to discover and creatively play. Each one of us has the unique potential to contribute to the creation of finite reality. What a glorious universe! Look around you and see all that we have already done! What a challenge, what an alluring adventure.

When we look up into the night sky, we see a wellnigh infinite myriad of stars—the evolutionary unfoldment of a mysterious majestic purpose. Our personalities are a driving force in the evolution of the universe, and the freedom of our choices and their consequences—both good and bad—are left to play out. It seems that the wisdom behind the fundamental laws of cause and effect in the universe naturally create this foundational law guaranteeing that freewill must act and function to survive. The mechanisms of the universe have decreed that this is a good and healthy environment for freewill, imperfect creatures like us to exercise our choices and to flex our freewill muscles—a finite environment of contrasts to choose from and to grow in.

The accumulation of evidence seems to suggest that there is a pattern to life, a meaningful purpose to evolution. When we find and understand the things that contribute to this pattern, we naturally look for a meaning to it, and where there is purpose and meaning we soon recognise that we need to look for the **value** of it all. As we map out our origins by observing patterns and joining the progressive dots, we observe the unfolding of the long evolution of life, going right back to the primitive warm inland seas where life on our earth earnestly began to develop. Then, onwards, to where these roots have given rise to the many branches of the incredible tree of life. We identify the branches that we originate from—those of our animal cousins. As we branched out along with the animals, we kept on branching out again, and again, and again, which finally culminated in a profound evolutionary mutational difference between us and the rest of life. A creature has evolved with the mental capacity to accommodate the workings of a consciousness of mind where freewill can choose to make a moral decision. We have the ability to transcend ourselves and this, along with the functioning of freewill, distinguishes us from the rest of the animal kingdom.

We have a consciousness; we are conscious of being conscious. We have the capacity and the ability to look before we leap. Because we are conscious of being conscious, our thinking minds can even observe ourselves; contemplate our own thoughts and actions from a higher perspective. Our mind is operated and directionally driven by the power and motives of our freewill choices. We now have the capacity to observe and discern the differences between the natural laws of the material universe that are made up of the law of cause and effect and realize the different outcomes that our freewill choices contribute to the creation of reality around us. Our evolution to freewill has given us a licence to participate in the creation of the finite universe! Our personality with its freewill is one of the prime movers in our world.

CHAPTER 1   17

A liberating and awesome responsibility worth celebrating!

CHAPTER 2

Discovering the Elements of Reflective Thinking

While collecting wood for his clan's night fire, something catches the eye of this primitive man. It's a weathered smooth piece of wood with a ball-like knob on the end of it (he has discovered another thing!) He then notices some facts about this "thing"; it's from an old weathered dead tree that's fallen over and been uprooted. It's about a metre long and is lying next to the ditch near the stump of the dead tree and is a broken off section of the root. He drops his pile of sticks that he's been collecting and picks up the weathered piece of wood. He then repeatedly slaps it into the palm of his hand. While he's doing this his mind starts to reason; he asks himself, "what could I do with this thing?" Then comes a light bulb moment—an enlightened idea! The dots are naturally and automatically joined in his thinking, and he suddenly realises what great value this piece of wood has. He could use this to defend himself or smash someone's skull in the neighbouring tribe. His natural disposition is distrustful, fear bulks large in his intellect as he instinctively knows they hate him;

they grunt differently and don't smell the same. His life is a fragile thing, surrounding him is an environment that relentlessly pushes him to think. It is unforgivingly harsh and dangerous. With these three steps his reflective mind has naturally connected the dots of the basic elements of reality: *"**fact, idea, and relation**"* (previously referred to as "**things**, **meanings**, and **values**.") This primitive man is standing on the shoulders of all the drivers—the instincts—of his animal cousins. This primitive savage is silhouetted in the awakening dawn—standing on the edge of the beginnings of the journey of evolving civilisation.

In making sense of this reality, our primitive man has arranged the pieces together in their place of his foundational framework for rational thinking without even knowing it. He saw a thing, got an idea, and once he realised the value of it… well that was the kicker; he was driven to act. Once we recognise and understand this simple framework, we find it is not that complex and is very workable. It is dependable and real! This fundamental framework is our personal arena of choice wherein our personality functions and choses to make decisions.

So, moving on into our modern world we can now say:

> "There are just three elements in universal reality: fact, idea, and relation. The religious consciousness identifies these realities as science, philosophy, and truth. Philosophy would be inclined to view these activities as reason, wisdom, and faith; physical reality, intellectual reality, and spiritual reality. We are in the habit of designating these realities as thing, meaning, and value." [2]

With this innate intuition of mind, human personality can creatively interact with these basic elements. Humans have within them the potential and freewill motivation to become, noble, inspiring, and wise over time. With accumulated knowledge, intuition, and foresight we can work towards becoming the most creative, caring, and enlightened personal creature on the face of the Earth. However, with unbridled selfishness, thoughtlessness, or just sheer laziness, we also have the ability to become a torment and menace to ourselves and others, even to the very Earth on which we live. No wonder primitive societies had so many taboos with "do nots" as their commandments. In early civilisation the fear of transgressing any of the taboos was an effective controlling mechanism, a brake to inhibit our unenlightened, uncontrolled primitive natural tendencies, an attempt to avoid the chaos of consequences. Fortunately, within the more progressive aspects of our modern civilisations we seem to be moving away from placing too much emphasis on the negative—"thou shalt not"—towards a more positive approach saying instead "you should because…"

Emerging Science, New Philosophies and Transition

The Renaissance and Enlightenment eras with their ongoing discoveries that brought on the scientific era, have had a tremendously positive effect on our way of thinking. The validity in the application of the scientific method for observing and analysing aspects of material reality has caused us to move forward in leaps and bounds. With increased knowledge and understanding we have successfully destroyed many erroneous beliefs and superstitions. However, in our transitioning and complex world there emerges an abundance of new possibilities many of which have resulted in philosophic confusion. Some elements of postmodernist thinking appear to be intellectually liberating but are missing the vital element of objective reality. The postmodernists advocate that there is no objective reality or truth outside of themselves; they advocate that everyone's subjective reality is valid, and this should be reflected in our social constructs. But the seeds of postmodernist thinking can't help but sprout into objective reality. The repercussions of subjective thinking will be reflected back onto us through its outworking in objective reality; this is nature's inbuilt reality-check to show us whether or not our subjective thinking contains the cohesiveness of truth. For thousands of years humanity has known the simple truth that "you reap what you sow".

Materialism has emerged in modern day philosophical thought. One modern school of scientific thought says that through reason and rational thinking we have successfully freed ourselves from the many superstitions, taboos, and outworn traditions of the past, therefore we no longer have any need for a belief in God. With our rapid advances in science, agnostic and atheistic thinking gradually emerged and increased in momentum during the twentieth century. This movement expounds that we can work it all out entirely by ourselves without needing a belief system and faith in the value of an unseen personal creator. It advocates that it is rational and sensible, therefore better, to disregard religious belief which can't be seen with the material eye and can't be proven by scientific methods. So, because most of the world's institutional religions promote traditions that many believe are just social constructs that leave little room for revision, the focus of postmodernists and materialists on outdated dogma and theology means that it should **all** be abandoned; throw out the lot—even if there is a baby in the bathwater! People who subscribe to this kind of thinking justify their stance by simply looking at all the terrible things humanity has done in the name of religion. They proclaim that it is no longer rational to present a faith in the existence of this kind of God to modern man, one which has so many inconsistencies in its ideas and ideals with concepts that don't ring true. So, belief and faith in even the possibility of the goodness of God is considered a fanciful illusion. They will go on to point out that "religion" is often used to excuse unholy activities and unfair judgement of others. They say that the positive aspects of religion sound nice but in reality, none of it is objectively real, therefore, it's not worth even postulating that there may exist a personal centre to all things and beings. No, they say, we are capable of working it all out on our own. We can work out our own meaning of things and can come up with all the necessary moral and ethical constructs wherein we can finally create our own sensible and sane set of values that are based on materialistic and subjective thinking.

Using this same line of thinking, the opposite can be argued; that we should look at the havoc that's eventuated because of our partial scientific discoveries in regard to material things. Think about the inventions, cannons, machine guns, atomic bombs, industrial pollution, disconnection from the natural world, noise pollution, climate change and buildings that scar the beauty of the earth. Then we could equally argue about what we've so recently gone and done with some of the postmodernist and materialistic "ideas" with philosophies and ideologies such as communism, fascism, anarchy, and nihilism.

Let's not forget, there are three basic elements in the workings of our mind; "fact, idea and relation", and it's these three intuitions "… that give objective validity, reality to man's experience in and with things, meanings and values." *[2]* So, in regard to facts—material things—they are right there in front of us. Science discovers the facts about **things** so that acquired knowledge can be put to creative practical use. Regarding ideas and how meaningful they are—this is not so clear as there are lots of ideas and, at times, they can be vague and fuzzy. Philosophy, through rational and reasoned thinking attempts to sift and sort these ideas giving them careful consideration in terms of their **meaning**; it tries to build the bridge between our understanding of things and values. Now regarding the relation between facts and ideas—between things and meanings—here is where we need to consider the **value** of what has been discovered and thought about. Here is where we look before we leap; where we decide on what are the best things to do with our ideas. This is where we venture out into the realms of faith in worthy values in terms of our decisions. This is where we draw on our value systems in terms of whether we will base our decisions on things that are true, beautiful, and good; on things that are of equal value to others.

When the primitive man first considered the value of that piece of wood with a knob on the end as being something he could use to crack open the skull of his enemy, his value decision was wholly motivated by his need to survive. For thousands of years evolving mankind was primarily driven with this struggle for survival. Later, as society became more advanced, humanity became preoccupied with improving its standard of living, therefore the motivation for deciding on the value of the plethora of ideas was based more upon materialistic needs. As society becomes more sophisticated and more content with material comforts, people have more time to think and ponder the bigger questions about life. Our humanity is struggling towards a quality of thought. As ideas about answers to the big questions about life emerge, the motivation for decision making needs to come from a good, balanced set of values.

Science, philosophy, and religion are all methods for finding truth. Ideally in society, they should all work in harmony with one another and not be at loggerheads. If not, we run the risk of becoming unbalanced. As an analogy, think of reality as being like a three-legged stool. If one leg of the stool is shorter than the other, or if one of the legs was missing the stool won't stand—it would be totally useless. If we ignore or place more value and emphasis on just one or two of these things leaving one or two of them out, we will end up with unstable and undesirable outcomes such as unbalanced and erroneous thinking causing erroneous assumptions; unsustainable ideologies causing fanaticism and conflict, intellectual snobbery, philosophical confusion, fanatical religious zeal and other forms of fanatical behaviour; incomplete and distorted views of reality; over-specialisation of viewpoints; the ugly side of materialism; and incomplete cosmologies. Further outcomes could be the bucket of blockers that spill over from an overly unrealistic estimation of things such as, self-importance, prejudice, resentment, and fear of the unknown. Not to mention the sometimes emotional, unpleasant experiences with the imperfections of ourselves and others that can block our enthusiasm for further exploration.

When those who subscribe to an atheistic way of thinking, are inclined to be critical about those who subscribe to a more religious way of thinking they need to be fair and balanced in their criticisms and realise that both schools of thought are actually on equal ground in terms of the validity of their arguments. Neither side can prove whether there is a God or not so more qualitative intelligent thought needs to be applied to the subject. Because most religious texts are ancient and deemed holy, therefore not open to revision, many outworn aspects of them have become easy targets to criticise from a position of accumulated modern-day facts but, in our criticism, are we taking into account the history of the circumstances.? Are we considering that there may be more to the meaning of "religion" than just institutional dogma? By studying history, we can assess whether the outcomes of certain ideas and ideals worked well or not—the proof is always in the pudding so to speak. In light of the given evolving circumstances, we may be right in the facts of many situations but wrong in the truth.

The modern scientific method of searching for truth by understanding facts in relation to material things is just one evolving aspect of the three elements of reality. It too, has a long and strange evolutionary history in reaching today's level of understanding. As scientific knowledge has evolved it has become more real and useful to us because much of what it deals with is tangible and can be proved. However, we need to be careful not to fall into the trap of jumping to the conclusion that just because science has advanced at a faster pace than the other methods of truth seeking, like philosophy and religion, that we can justify pooh-haring everything else.

> "The ancients sought a supernatural explanation for all natural phenomena not within the range of their personal comprehension; and many moderns continue to do this. The depersonalization of so-called natural phenomena has required ages, and it is not yet completed. But the frank, honest, and fearless search for true causes gave birth to modern science: It turned astrology into astronomy, alchemy into chemistry, and magic into medicine." [2]

Modern day scientists would shake their heads and laugh at certain aspects of the early pioneers of their professions. The same can be said about the early pioneers of rational thought and ancient religionists. The quest for truth is innate in human nature and some truths are easier to discover, grasp, and express than others. Proof of the physical nature of the material world should not be considered the only criteria for accepting greater truth about the things we recognise as being real yet cannot see or touch, and that cannot be put under a microscope to be viewed and analysed by scientific methods. Let's remember that, in the innate workings of mind, our understanding and insights are evolving and growing.

Society at large seems to be overwhelmed by too much information and is hesitant to take a deeper interest in the fundamental purpose and progress of our personal and collective philosophical thinking and, even more so, in our religious ideas and ideals. But one must continue to ask the question—how is all this playing out in the complex reality of our modern world? The ugly side of materialism showed its face in the first half of the twentieth century where humanity experienced an horrendous and violent clash of ideologies as a result of the pursuit of a plethora of modern-day ideas for building utopian societies such as communism, fascism, and anarchy. We saw how we were all at each other's throats, contributing to the ghastly global atrocities that resulted in hundreds of millions of deaths of innocent people and unbelievable destruction. With the accumulation of knowledge modern society is now in a position of transition from one stage of civilisation to the next.

The Scientific Method and Postmodernism

What is the scientific method?
(Excerpt from Encyclopaedia Britannica):

"The scientific method is critical to the development of scientific theories, which explain empirical (experiential) laws in a scientifically rational manner. In a typical application of the scientific method, a researcher develops a hypothesis, tests it through various means, and then modifies the hypothesis on the basis of the outcome of the tests and experiments. The modified hypothesis is then retested, further modified, and tested again, until it becomes consistent with observed phenomena and testing outcomes. In this way, hypotheses serve as tools by which scientists gather data. From that data and the many different scientific investigations undertaken to explore hypotheses, scientists are able to develop broad general explanations, or scientific theories." [5]

What do postmodernists believe?
(Excerpt from an article on Postmodernists by Brian Duignan, a senior editor at Encyclopaedia Britannica. His subject areas include philosophy, law, social science, politics, political theory, and religion):

"Many postmodernists hold one or more of the following views: (1) there is no objective reality; (2) there is no scientific or historical truth (objective truth); (3) science and technology (and even reason and logic) are not vehicles of human progress but suspect instruments of established power; (4) reason and logic are not universally valid; (5) there is no such thing as human nature (human behaviour and psychology are socially determined or constructed); (6) language does not refer to a reality outside itself; (7) there is no certain knowledge; and (8) no general theory of the natural or social world can be valid or true (all are illegitimate 'metanarratives')." [6]

It is important to note that postmodernists don't necessarily hold all of these views, however they may believe in one or more, or a combination, of them.

More from Brian Duignan:

"1. There is an objective natural reality, a reality whose existence and properties are logically independent of human beings—of their minds, their societies, their social practices, or their investigative techniques. Postmodernists dismiss this idea as a kind of naive realism. Such reality as there is, according to postmodernists, is a conceptual construct, an artefact of scientific practice and language. This point also applies to the investigation of past events by historians and to the description of social institutions, structures, or practices by social scientists.

"2. The descriptive and explanatory statements of scientists and historians can, in principle, be objectively true or false. The postmodern denial of this viewpoint—which follows from the rejection of an objective natural reality—is sometimes expressed by saying that there is no such thing as Truth...." [6]

CHAPTER 2

And finally, here are two short definitions of aspects of postmodernism copied from Wikipedia:

"Postmodernists are generally 'sceptical of explanations which claim to be valid for all groups, cultures, traditions, or races' and describe truth as relative. It can be described as a reaction against attempts to explain reality in an objective manner by claiming that reality is a mental construct."

"Many postmodern claims are a deliberate repudiation of certain 18th-century Enlightenment values. Such a postmodernist believes that logic and reason are mere conceptual constructs that are not universally valid. Postmodernists also believe there are no objective moral values. A postmodernist then tolerates multiple conceptions of morality, even if he or she disagrees with them subjectively. Postmodern writings often focus on deconstructing the role that power and ideology play in shaping discourse and belief. Postmodern philosophy shares ontological similarities with classical sceptical and relativistic belief systems." [7]

It might be helpful to further explore the philosophic confusion and the void that has been created by the effects of both scientific materialism and postmodernist lines of thinking and the influence they have had on the thinking of our modern-day humanity. My understanding is that while scientific materialism observes and acknowledges that we experience and interact with objective material reality, postmodernists believe that there is no objective reality. Well, that puts my head in a spin... Although postmodernism says there are no moral or ethical values to observe that lie outside of ourselves, therefore subjective reality is all that counts, and scientific materialism is dependent on objective reality to conclude on its factual discoveries, both have a tendency to conclude that the creation of the universe, the first cause of everything, is purely material and mechanical; there is no personality in a first cause. Then the postmodernist line of thinking believes that because there exists no external, objective reality, no morality, ethics, or known values outside of themselves, everything is simply a construct of our inner subjective mind. They believe they have intellectually freed themselves from social constructs and constraints and feel liberated to be whoever they want to be, and that others also have the right to believe whatever they wish to believe. Some even go on to advocate there is no truth outside of themselves which the materialistic scientist completely and absolutely disagrees with.

Aspects of these ideas have filtered into, and float around in, our modern world. However, I believe there is a vital coherent element to both of these lines of thinking that is missing. As we say, a little knowledge can be a dangerous thing. We are living in challenging times. In the history of humanity, we are living in an era like no other. The transitioning from one stage to another has created that void and somehow, we need to move forward and through the void. Humanity must put forth greater efforts in identifying and utilizing all elements available to our minds that will help to produce a foundation for the function of a quality of thinking. Humanity needs to equip itself with the sharpened tools of understanding and insight to rid itself of this pit that is being filled with philosophic confusion.

The search for truth by using the scientific method—by developing a philosophy based on the outcomes of the analysis of observable known facts—has effectively de-personalised and destroyed much that is unworthy for the enlightened age we live in. Now we are in a better position to observe the evolution of human thought as it slowly emerged from primitive fear and ignorance. In an effort to make sense of the world around them, we now understand that our primitive ancestors personalised and humanised almost everything that was a mystery to them—everything that couldn't be explained—even their concepts of deity. They attributed things such as thunder and lighting, famines and floods, good and bad luck, and everything else unexplained, to the spirit world of ghosts and gods. A friend once jokingly said to me, "God made man in His image, and then man promptly returned the favour." But, in viewing the early and later religious evolution of values and formulated beliefs, it is important to note that embedded within these humans was a fundamental urge and necessity to move towards the pursuit of morals and values. Regardless of questioning the validity of past beliefs, when we view them from the perspective of our modern world and when we view our ancestors' taboos—their do's and don'ts and their stories—we observe they contain moral lessons and emerging values which have contributed greatly to the development of the very civilisation in which we now stand and in which we have the humble privilege to view our past in regard to these endeavours.

> "Man evolved through the superstitions of mana, magic, nature worship, spirit fear, and animal worship to the various ceremonials whereby the religious attitude of the individual became the group reactions of the clan. And then these ceremonies became focalized and crystallized into tribal beliefs, and eventually these fears and faiths became personalized into gods. But in all of this religious evolution the moral element was never wholly absent." [2]

So...

> "Rationalism is wrong when it assumes that religion is at first a primitive belief in something which is then followed by the pursuit of values. Religion is primarily a pursuit of values, and then there formulates a system of interpretative beliefs." [2]

The scientific materialist's belief that the universe was created purely by material means has been based on the modern scientific method. This has been widely considered to be a logical belief system without taking into account the creativity of personality as being a core attribute to the creation of our reality. However, a technical analysis in and of itself does not reveal what a person or even a thing is capable of doing. Take for example an analysis of the chemical elements that go towards the composition of water; one (hydrogen) is highly explosive and the other (oxygen) freely burns. You could never predict the outcome through analysis of these separate components that their combination in the form of H_2O would produce an entirely new substance such as liquid water that would actually extinguish fire! [2] The outcome of such a methodical analysis can be completely erroneous! We will examine this in more depth in the coming chapters.

All the elements that go toward making up our physical life—including our minds, freewill, and personality—must have origins derived from a first cause. You could take a snapshot in time of our observations in regard to the formation of life in the universe and say, "we have observed that life as we know it only exists on our planet, therefore it looks as though we are alone in the universe and just an evolutionary accident." But with the accumulation of more facts that give us a greater understanding, this radically changes the picture, rendering the previous conclusions as being partial and completely wrong.

According to Kepler space mission data, astronomers reported in November 2013 that there could be as many as 40 billion Earth-sized planets orbiting in the habitable zones of Sun-like stars and red dwarfs in the Milky Way. And that's just in our Milky Way galaxy! One 2016 study estimated that the observable universe contains two trillion—or two million million—galaxies. So that's 40 billion times the two trillion Earth-sized planets orbiting in the habitable zones of Sun-like stars in our galaxy! As of the first of December 2022, there are 5,284 confirmed exoplanets, the majority of which were discovered by the Kepler space telescope. With this new evidence of exoplanets, we can now rationally surmise through statistical analysis that the evolution of life throughout this grand universe of two trillion galaxies is not so accidental after all. Life is important and has a part to play in contributing to the evolution and outcomes of not only individual planets such as ours but also this time-space universe as a whole. Whether we like it or not we play a part. The statistical possibility that the universe is teeming with life is very probable!

On 24 October 1946, rocket scientists captured the first images of Earth taken from space. The photo was black and white and not much of a view. But then in 1968, along with millions of other people, I remember, as a child, seeing for the very first time what our Earth really looked like from space. Most memorable for me was the "Earthrise" shot taken by the astronauts orbiting the Moon; to me it showed the sheer beauty and fragility of Earth, and how insignificantly small we appeared in our vast universe home.

We are inquisitive creatures, and because of that we have acquired insight and learned much. Our primitive man first joined the dots between a fact (the piece of wood), an idea (what he could do with that piece of wood), and the relationship between them causing him to realise the value of what he'd discovered. In similar fashion, using the same innate function of the mind, we have learned by experience to do sophisticated and even amazing things. Take Eratosthenes the Greek for example—he was a mathematician and head of the library at Alexandria. Simply by observing the shadows cast by the sun on two sticks planted in the ground at two different points he formulated the equation for figuring out the circumference of our world—a man 2,200 years ago found the circumference of our entire planet with just a stick and his mind! Incredible!

Ok, let's leave some of these things we have just touched upon hanging for the time being and explore them a little deeper in the following chapters. For now, I'd like to reiterate where we've come so far in exploring the foundational processes of human thinking. Here is a formula for the evolving human side of our intuitive thinking minds: fact + idea + relation = things, meanings, and values. This is the basic way our material human mind creatively works.

In the following chapters we will explore the personal subjective aspects of our relationship to the universe in which we live and attempt to untangle some of the complications of our thinking processes. We will look more closely into the "relational" aspects of our thinking. It is within this relational aspect that we will attempt to discover new elements that emerge from within our accumulated experiences of working with the basic elements of facts, ideas, and their relationship. Can these emerging elements be observed and analysed to find out whether or not we can include them into our foundational framework of thinking? Emerging elements must be just as real in our engagement with finite reality and just as vital to our thinking as the others that have already been outlined. They will be the ones we may not be fully utilising, yet ones that will be a vital ingredient producing a solid foundation for our individuality and be necessary elements to improve our creativity and quality of thinking.

As we head off into the unchartered waters of life, we are equipped with a free will and a mind that contains a compass of truth. I believe we all have an innate sense of what truth is. A single great truth can be presented in a story or parable; by analysing the story and its parts we can each come up with many different interpretations and applications which in itself can be a worthwhile process. However, they are not necessarily in and of themselves revealing the actual meaning of the great truth found in the story. The trick is to grasp the actual meaning of the truth. The beauty of the meaning of a truth is that it can be understood, appreciated, and shared by multiple individuals who don't all think the same way. The books, songs, plays, and movies that tend to be most memorable to people are the ones that contain meaningful stories and insights into truth. For example, what is the meaning of the great truth presented in "The Good Samaritan"? *[8]*

CHAPTER 3

The Emerging Relational Elements—Our Value System

In the late 1960's next to the neighbourhood where I grew up, there was an old, abandoned gold mining site dating back to the 1850's. It was located in the hills and valleys of a place called Warrandyte. I used to go there with my best friend who everyone called Titch. We were around fourteen years of age and both enthusiastic for adventure. Titch was a small guy; his older brother and parents were small in height too. His dad rode a racing pushbike with fixed pedals and no brakes, which I thought was a little crazy. His dad also had a boxing ring set up in his double garage where he trained the local kids. Anyway, Titch and I used to spend weekends away camping and exploring the shafts and mines that were scatted throughout the Warrandyte hills and valleys. The place had become very over-grown; it hadn't been touched since the end of the gold rush in 1890, so we had to be careful not to fall down any of the abandoned shafts. To set off on our adventures all we needed to take with us was a tent, sleeping bags, a billy, two torches and lots of candles. We didn't need to take any food because the crystal clear fresh-water creeks that flowed through the valleys provided us with clean drinking water and an abundance of yabbies. (Yabbies look like a cross between a large prawn and a small lobster, and they are delicious; two or three of them boiled for five minutes in the billy were enough for a tasty meal.)

At first light we would head off to search the hills for mines and shafts. Some of the bigger mines went into the hills for a kilometre or so, with many tunnels branching off them. We soon discovered that the tunnels were always following a seam of white quartz that contained all the gold that was to be found. The miners relentlessly chased these seams of quartz. Sometimes we would shine the torch through the darkness up onto the roof and we'd see that nearly fifty feet up, right at the top, was a thin line of quartz in the middle of the roof. There were a lot of other tunnels going off these main shafts as well which followed other veins of quartz. Quite often they didn't go very far because the vein had simply run out. Some shafts went straight down from the floor and were filled with water with wobbly wooden planks over them. We did find some gold once and were full of excitement, but it turned out to be just fool's gold. As a kid I was amazed at the lengths and the sheer amount of time and effort humans put into finding things that are so rare and valuable.

Just like the miners digging and panning for gold, this section is aimed at looking for the **emerging golden elements** that are mostly hidden from our limited view. They can be discovered within through the living of our lives, and they become observable in the fruits of our interactions with objective reality.

These emerging golden elements are potential and can grow from within our relational/value element of our thinking. They can also continue to emerge and become more real as we accumulate knowledge, develop ideas, and learn and grow from experiences. They emerge through our successes and failures and how we respond to the everyday struggles of life. They emerge in the way we reflect upon our decisions and realise how we can become better at living. However, these emerging elements may differ from, or even conflict with, our animalistic wants and desires that come from within the basic elements of thinking illustrated by the primitive man story. If we are driven by a desire to improve our way of living the emerging elements simply reveal themselves to us. When we start to place a lot of value on the more positive aspects of living, we soon realise that these emerging value elements are in fact the important values of **truth, beauty, and goodness**. We come to this conclusion simply by identifying what happens when we apply them in our everyday lives; when we experience and observe how more meaningful life can be and how much better we feel in our inner lives. These golden emerging elements of our thinking are the non-material values that sit neatly upon, and relate beautifully to, those three basic elements of reality that we have already discussed as being things, meanings, and values. This second layer of a threefold elemental value system greatly enhances our insights to enable us to engage creatively with the basic elements as we link them together to help us grow towards worthwhile values.

As already stated, the mind is like a musical instrument. There is a simplicity to its structure, but upon this structure can be brought forth a wellnigh infinite number of melodies; you can write thousands of songs by just playing three chords. The human will can choose to learn and play the uplifting melodies of relational harmonics. Once we learn how the mind works and what it is capable of, our ear can become attuned to the emerging elements making it easier to avoid playing too many wrong notes. Do we want to create lives like a recurring cacophony of sound or like a beautiful melodic symphony? The emerging elements of reality appear in the decision-making aspect of our thinking process.

We are personalities (therefore personal), and we have a relationship with reality and the people around us. When we think about the basic elements, we discover that our thinking is driven by the interrelationship between those three elements. Everything about our thinking has to do with evaluating this interrelationship that makes us decide on our choices of action or reaction to every bit of reality we perceive within and around us. In other words, we choose to place a "relationship value" on everything. When we decide what our *values* are, this will drive our ideas and ideals—our relationship to things and meanings, which in turn make us self-conscious of our values. The proof of our values is reflected in our interactions with the surrounding environment and our relationships with others. Because we are personal, our personal identity sits in the realm of our values. So what drives us as we sit on the throne of our personal seat of identity? What is our "value driver"?

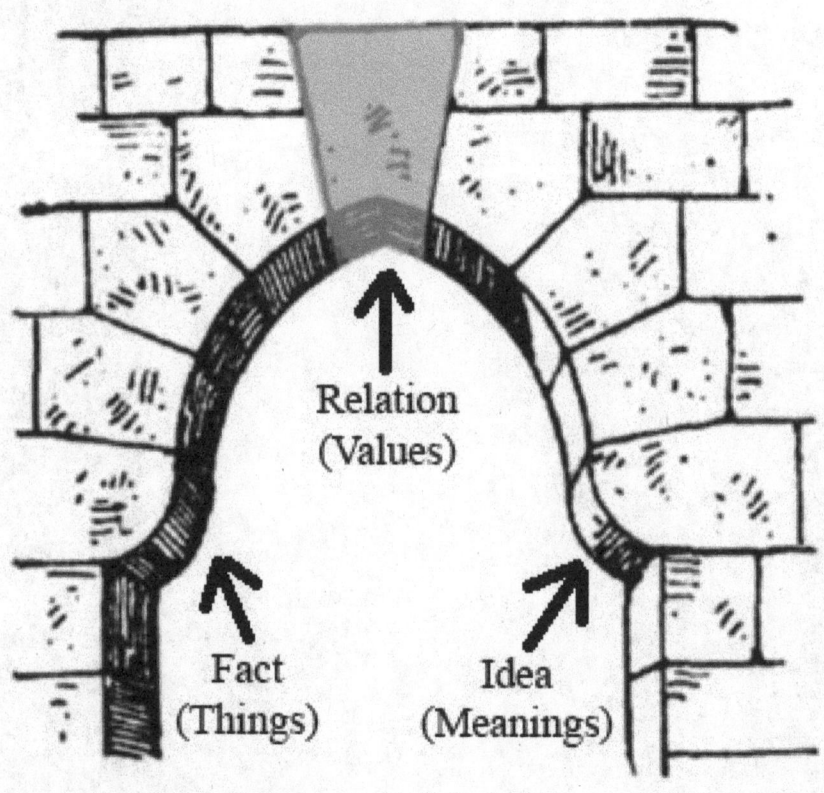

Finding the Keystone—the Value-Driver of Choice

What is a keystone? When building an archway, a keystone is the wedge-shaped stone at the summit of the arch. It is the final stone placed during construction and locks all the other stones into position, allowing the arch to bear the weight. It is something on which associated things depend, hence the term "the keystone of one's philosophy."

In making sense of our evolving perception of reality we have, in a sense, started to build a 'foundational archway' that supports the basis of our thinking. We have been placing the stones and cementing the basic elements of reality together to be our 'framework for thinking'. Carrying this archway analogy forwarded, we now need to find and understand the "keystone" to our foundational archway because this is the essential stone that is to take all the weight, for within this keystone our value systems are emerging and growing.

It also may be helpful to view this archway as our personal front door, our humble but grand entrance where our motivations interact with reality. It is through this foundational archway of thinking where our perception of objective reality enters, and where it gets processed and interpreted and plays itself out according to our subjective reality and our individual choices. As we grow in this way, so do we build our living abode wherein we collect our galleries of facts, ideas, and interpretations along with our memories and experiences that build up a reality within us that we can rely on. A key aspect to all of this is to understand that our personal **freewill** functions within this realm of the keystone of our archway.

So, as we build our emerging foundation to create a place where we will be living and acting in our daily lives, let's ask ourselves, have we got it all together? Is our keystone strong enough? In other words, have we sorted out our system of values? As I mentioned before, our value system evolves and grows within the keystone—it is the substance of the keystone. The strength and quality of any keystone relies on its properties. Therefore, our value systems need to be carefully examined and scrutinized because it is the placement of values in their order of importance in the keystone that will determine what we ultimately think and do. The outcomes of our actions will determine and reveal exactly what we value.

So, does our value system serve us well? For example, if you place more *value* on the possession of *things* (e.g., the love of money) than on how you treat other people, the *meaning* of that could play out to look something like, "I come first, I look after myself regardless of anything else. I'll even take advantage of you to get more of the things I want. Sorry pal, that's just the way the world works. Because I value my things, I have decided they are more important to me than you." Regardless of the ethical and moral aspects of thinking and acting in that manner, this example illustrates that the nature of our value driver motivating the direction of our thinking and actions is determined by the placement of values in our keystone. Therefore, it's the positioning of values in our keystone that we need to focus on and carefully examine, for this is what determines what kinds of people we will be and how our lives will play out. It's where and how we position our values that provides the key to determining what drives our choices. Once we understand the nature and importance of the value-driver we can examine the emerging elements that make up the keystone within our thinking process.

The mind can view reality on different levels, and it does this through the value keystone. Over time humans appreciate more and more the emerging values of **truth**, **beauty**, and **goodness** because **"truth is coherent, beauty is attractive**, and **goodness is stabilizing"**. *[2]* It is through these emerging realities that we create our ideas of human ethics, morals, and values. By including them into our "value keystone" we give them power to renew our motivation—to be driven by these emerging gems. For example, if we choose to be willingly motivated by—to value—truth, beauty, and goodness, and add these elemental gems to our understanding of "things, meanings and values," we thereby recognise their significance in contributing to outcomes—we place them above all other values. This means we choose to value these important emerging elements over our lesser self-serving values when and if they differ. We probably do this already to varying degrees as we think and make choices, but by simply understanding how the keystone value driver works in our thinking process, we can become more conscious of incorporating these higher values when we make our decisions. The most important thing of all to decide in life is just what the hell it is that we want to build within this supporting foundational archway anyway? We need to think about this because it is where we will be living out our future—where our seat of identity will be.

To us as individuals these elements are crucial, as they contribute to our wellbeing by unifying our personality and because, again, truth is coherent, beauty is attractive, and goodness is stabilizing. They are like vitamins contained in a healthy balanced diet that boost the immune system of our thinking. They help ward off dysfunctional diseases of the mind.

Early on in evolution humanity came to the realisation that we are incomplete—we are imperfect. The realisation of this gives us the ability to decide how to position our emerging values towards a higher value—an ideal—that we can envision as being perfect. The universe gives us the time-tensions between imperfection and perfection because it gives us experience. Contained in our relationship to the universe are the things of value to be discovered. The emerging golden elements contribute to the strengthening of the consistency of our developing keystone that contributes toward a mind that can attain a higher quality of thinking.

The basic practical value of those necessary material things of the world are, of course, important, but much of it, when viewed from a personal value level can be considered merely as essential scaffolding needed to function effectively in our daily life. On this higher, non-material level of emerging values our real personal growth happens which in turn places more importance on our relationship to others. Also, these emerging values greatly assist our creativity in what we do with material reality. The values we discover through these experiences, I believe, are of lasting value.

There is a co-dependency or interrelationship of everything in the universe for everything to exist. For example, our solar system needs a sun to hold everything in place; the diversity of life on our world relies on water for its existence. To maintain stability, growth, and continuity there is a dependency between life and its environment. Even for our thinking mind to maintain stability and growth it has a dependency on the recognition of the emergence of the values of truth, beauty, and goodness.

Surely, after roughly a million years of evolution, the human race has accumulated enough experience to examine and seriously address the following questions: Wouldn't it be wise to pause and consider just what kind of building we need to create within? What are we attempting to build here in our minds that will be creatively reflected in our external lives? Should we not strive for a living building of creativity to be made of, and to be reflective of, the emergence of the coherent truth of things, the lure of the attractive beauty in meanings, and the quest towards the attainment of the stabilisation of the goodness in values? Can we agree on this?

"To say that mind 'emerged' from matter explains nothing. If the universe were merely a mechanism and mind were unapart from matter, we would never have two differing interpretations of any observed phenomenon. The concepts of truth, beauty, and goodness are not inherent in either physics or chemistry. A machine cannot know, much less know truth, hunger for righteousness, and cherish goodness." [2]

Our civilisation is in a unique position. Just like individuals who have reached a certain age of maturity and discernment when they can look back on their lives while at the same time looking forward in the planning of their future—so too it is with civilisation. In our adventure of life, if we disregard the already discovered and emerging values of beauty, truth, and goodness in our value keystone, how would we attempt to ensure that decisions about our aims in life are sustainable enough to safeguard our direction? What would we draw on to sustain us when the 'well of human insight' seems to have run dry? How would we position and correctly define our goals to keep us stable? How would we create and sustain an equable, just, and fair society? How would we protect the freedoms and rights of each individual? How would we create environments that are conducive to the attractiveness of beauty? How would we avoid the mediocrity of the uniformity of thought or the anarchy of unbridled self-liberty? Would we leave our children to choose all their morals and ethical thinking without any nurturing of a value system inherited from their parents? Has the universe completely left us alone without assistance in using these value-elements? These are questions we will ask and attempt to explore in more detail in the coming chapters.

It's interesting to note that when we analyse the philosophies that gave origin to our institutions of learning and governance, we observe that they are derived, and have evolved from understandings gleaned over time from experiences relating to the higher-minded value systems of truth, beauty, and goodness. All of our great human endeavours in regard to science, philosophy, political systems, and value concepts of the world's religions took root from our evolving understanding of the importance of these values. The great step taken when certain societies decided to separate church and state—separation of the governance of laws from theological institutions—is an indication of how societies evolve and develop through experiential insights gained from trial and error when observing how certain ideas play out in the real world.

The only way we have achieved these leaps and bounds in our evolutionary history is because of the remarkable fact that our minds are endowed with innate qualities that aid us in becoming competent at discriminating between truth and error, right and wrong, and fairness and injustice. The recognition of the higher emerging values gives us the very ability to recognise the "truth" in relationship to "things, meanings, and values" (the basic elements of reality.) This ability to recognise truth is the very basis of science and philosophy. It also gives us the intellectual foundation of genuine religion. Beauty is recognised by the intellect allowing us to appreciate the existence and attraction of beauty. The recognition of beauty sponsors the creativity of music, art, and the meaningful rhythms of human experience. Through our mind endowments we can also become aware of the truth in relation to the importance of the stability of goodness. This sense of goodness enables us to formulate and improve our ethics, morality, and religion—our hunger to experience perfection.

We also have the ability to recognise the relativity of values. We have an innate understanding of the significance and position of values as they work with the three basic elements. We can recognise that the basic elements are inter-related with the emerging elements. These two sets of elements—the first in experiential existence and the other with potential emergence—function nicely together in our minds. With this enlightened understanding, the human connotations of the word "religion" need to be re-defined to fit into this context of emergence; religious values are related to the intellectual foundations of the truth of science and philosophy—they are not something completely separate. All these emerging relationships are becoming reality, they are essential, they are beneficial value-relational elements that unify an individual's thinking and creativity.

Civilisation will always be moving forward, and in the periods of change from one phase to the next—within these transition stages—we are always faced with the real possibility of a breakdown of cohesiveness within societies. To sustain a growing and changing society, civilisation needs to discover, recognise, and adopt a lasting value that is easily understood and is common to all—one that provides the cohesiveness needed to tie people together and to sustain them throughout the potentially turbulent upheavals of a forward moving civilisation. It will need to contain an element that gives a sense of belonging and purpose—one which supports, drives, and sustains real aspirations, values, and goals. A lasting cohesiveness will not be found within a uniformity of thought—by expecting everyone to think the same. That is simply unsustainable because each one of us is uniquely different. Humanity must discover the cohesiveness that is contained within a "unity of spirit" as opposed to a "uniformity of thought". Humanity needs to discern what this unity of spirit is. Once discovered, grasped, and understood this spirit will provide a real potential to sustain civilisation. More on this later.

The logic of science concludes that everything materially observable in our universe has eventuated from a first cause. But through the observation of this observation, it also becomes obvious that everything observable cannot come into existence from absolutely nothing; something does not and cannot come from nothing. The reason of philosophy backs up this basic logic. Reason reminds science that everything living in the material universe, including personality and the consciousness of mind and freewill—must also have eventuated from a first cause for it too is an observable reality in the universe. So, in the contemplation of first causes we must be mindful that **all** aspects of life are needed for personalities to function in a life vehicle. For us to function and exist in the universe, it stands to reason that if we, as persons, have evolved from the machinations of this first cause, **then personality and creativity must be inherent in, and be at the very core of such a first cause.** Following on from this line of reasoning, philosophy points out that the first thought of creativity can only originate from, and come into existence by, the act of a primal personality. If nothing comes from nothing, then everything must come from something, therefore personality must be existent in the first cause. The first cause must be, at the very least, a personality—but is infinitely more than that. The reason of philosophy should conclude that when all is said and done, creation by a first cause is, in the final analysis a **personal act**. Personality and creativity cannot be divorced from one another; personality cannot be divorced from a first creative cause; personality is the only observable primary element; it is the only observable cause of all creativity.

In this section we have identified the motivating driver—our relational keystone that contains the emerging triune value elements that are made up our ideas and ideals of beauty, truth, and goodness that sit and function within our value keystone. The beauty of the living instrument of our mind is that it functions in the same way in relation to these emerging perceptions as it innately functioned within the primitive humans. Our minds are well equipped for our evolutionary journey.

On the surface of things, it may seem that we have collected and identified all the needed elements that will contribute to creative and qualitative thinking. However, there is a higher cohesive value that is still missing. This missing piece of the jigsaw will position the priority of our values into a cohesive system that will unify the elements of our thinking processes. By finding and adding this last value—the origin of all true values—to the mix, I believe we will have discovered a new beginning—an enlightened moment. It has the potential to become the life-giving core of our existence. It will emanate as the highest value in our keystone. It will be the value of values that causes all other values to find their place. It will act as the master value of all our other values.

"Life is really simple, but we insist on making it complicated."
– *Confucius* [4]

My father, Frank Swadling & father-in-law, Henry Ward

CHAPTER 4

Our Quest for the Highest Value

When I was a teenager, I was naturally influenced by other people. I had my heroes, and in my own way, readily imitated them. All those people I looked up to and identified with influenced my sense of what I valued. Friends I gravitated towards were ones I got ideas from; my ideals were emerging, and my sense of values were changing and adjusting. It was a new and exciting time of changes and, upon reflection, in many ways an unconscious growth and adjustment in my thinking.

My wife's father was born in Yorkshire, England in 1911. He had two brothers; one was his identical twin who was, sadly, shot in battle during World War II by a sniper in Sicily after he tragically stuck his head up from inside a tank to look around. The other brother, the oldest of the three, became a minister in the Church of England early on in his career. My father-in-law was a wonderful man; he had a gifted temperament which made him naturally interested in others. He was one of those people who knew how the world worked; he was a balanced and thoughtful person but quite indignant towards human greed, while at the same time being understanding and compassionate towards the foibles of human nature. When he was a young man, he left England and sailed off to British North Borneo (now known as Sabah) where he worked for a tobacco company as an overseer of their tobacco plantations. Each year he took his vacations in Australia and while there, he met and fell in love with his wife-to-be at the Hydro Majestic which was a grand old hotel situated on an escarpment overlooking the Blue Mountains. When the Japanese invaded Borneo he was interned in a civilian prisoner of war camp where he became malnourished and nearly died of starvation. After the war ended, he returned to Australia to look for his long-lost love. They found each other, but not having heard from him and thinking he had died, she had become engaged to another fellow. When she realised my father-in-law was alive, and when they both realised that they were still in love, she promptly returned the ring to the other fellow and married my father-in-law.

They went on to have a long and loving relationship with a family of five gifted but very different talented girls. I first met my father-in-law when he was in his 70's. My wife and I renovated an old barn down the back of his property and turned it into a lovely home. Over the years I became close friends with him; he was easy to talk to and we would discuss all manner of subjects. I remember one balmy evening after dinner, we were sitting outside finishing our glasses of red wine, and, near the end of our conversation, he was telling me about his older brother who had become a minister of the Church of England. He was expressing how he just didn't have any faith in anything like his brother did; he was saying he would literally have to be struck by lighting and hear the thundering voice of God before he would believe in all that stuff. Throughout his life he never was struck by lightning; he never did "see the light." He couldn't understand how his brother always had faith, and he expressed how he wished he could have faith in something. In our conversation, I said that he must value *something* that he could have faith in. He thought about this for quite a while and then said, "Yes I do; I have faith in the goodness of love. I said to him, "Well there you go, that's something real and worthy enough to have faith in" and we clicked

CHAPTER 4

our glasses and finished our last drop of wine. Looking back on this conversation, it was one of those memorable moments when he realised that he did have a faith, and I think it was confirmed for him because he had experienced love—he had felt this love within. It was an insightful moment for me too.

"Love is the desire to do good to others." [2]

The goodness of love is the property of the human race because it belongs to everyone and is in everyone. Can we experience love in the absence of another personality? Is the ideal and adventure of romance and of sharing love with others, even possible without personality? No, I don't believe so; I think it would be meaningless. You can't put love under a microscope. Without love, relationships would just be an exercise in self-display simply to attract the opposite sex. In nature we observe this basic enthusiastic display among our animal cousins as we see them strutting around displaying the raw aspects of sex attraction. Within the higher species of mammals, we also observe amazing maternal instincts. The instincts of attraction and affection, along with the maternal instinct, lay the foundation for creatures like us to grasp and appreciate this higher value of love—to put our best foot forward so to speak, but these basic instincts and drivers are not the actual "element" of true love.

Love Is an Empty Vessel Unless It is Shared

The word "love" is used in a myriad of ways from "I love ice cream and hamburgers" to "I'm madly in love with you and want to marry you." Because of this it can be tricky talking and thinking about love, but let's just put aside any trivial usages of the word for a moment and quietly look within ourselves and think about the truth contained in the goodness of love. What are the fundamental attributes of true love? When I try really hard to nail down an answer to this question, all my limited experience and insight show me that the fundamental elements of love boil down to the three wonderfully personal interrelated elements of beauty, truth, and goodness which, in my mind, initiate a selfless quality of love and the motivation for "the desire to do good to others" kind of love. When you love someone, when you truly love someone, the feeling is real; once experienced it never leaves you. True love motivates you; it literally has the power to transform you in a positive way. We naturally adopt and personally embrace these kinds of ideals—these higher values—into our lives based on our personal experiences; we can experience that upswelling sensation of joy—we can even fall in love with Love itself.

When I dig a little deeper into the phenomenon of true love, I find that the interesting thing about the emerging elements of love is that they have wonderful and endless repercussions, because they have a real ongoing and un-ending relationship to all things, meanings, and values. In individuals and society, for example, they have the power to balance the profit motive with a genuine service motive. As we grow in our understanding and appreciation of values that are true, beautiful, and good we grow strong roots for the foundation of a more enduring civilisation. We discover that the creativity contained in love can never be exhausted. As we have freewill and are endowed with mind, personalities like us have been given the opportunity to function in the universe and to participate in its evolution.

CHAPTER 4

The more we are driven by the goodness of love the more valuable and lasting will our contributions be towards evolving creation. This goodness of love can only be expressed through personality—it cannot exist without personality. It would not be real and could not be experienced, created, discovered, expressed, or shared without personality. And it is only ever revealed to us through our relationships with other personalities! The proof of love's existence is revealed to us by experiencing its value. All our personalities, freewill, consciousness, creativity, and the endless relationship of love to reality could not possibly come from nothing. Therefore, love's creational core, its origin, **has to be personal**.

The unique thing about this love and its emerging elements compared to the basic elements of our thinking is that there is something eternal and timeless about them. When you put aside your material wants and desires and think about what is the most important value to you—what honestly is the highest value you can think of—like my father-in-law, most people will answer that it is the goodness contained in true love. They will willingly acknowledge that this love is the highest and most worthy of values because of the simple fact that it can be felt within them. Sometimes it's hard to express these feelings because this love often lies too deep for words.

And herein lies a great mystery and truth; the more a person approaches reality through the motivation of the goodness of love the greater the reality—the actuality—of that person.

The human personality is unconditionally creative; there is no creativity without personality and there is also no expression or sharing of love without a person. Our personality with its freewill is the prime mover in our world, so I don't have a problem accepting that the first cause to all finite reality has, at least at its core, primacy of personality as a creative attribute. The primal personality is the first creative cause. Personality is the prime mover in the universe! And this first cause relationship with all other future personalities

I believe must be a relationship of Love. I think that the will of creation can be found in our quest for the highest value in the universe.

If the first cause relationship to personality is the goodness of love, then these habits and laws of Love and their elements of reality can be discovered in the universe—they are there just waiting for our personalities to find and experience. How else could we begin to discover these vital elements that maintain our freewill and individuality and allow for the growth of our creative thinking? The mystery of the first cause is much more than just personality and love, but it can't be anything less! A first cause, therefore, must come with personal attributes and motivation. A first cause also contains within it the entire original source-pattern of creation that includes elements that emanate from their core of Love. Let's call them "spirit realities" as they need a title because we don't view them the same way as material realities; we can't literally see them; we experience their goodness through the eyes of our minds and in our emotional relationship with love's goodness that we feel to be true within our hearts. Spirit realities have an innate ability to enhance our value structures of thinking. We can view and feel them in the acts of others and of ourselves, and we can also materially observe them in the interaction of our creativity with the physical reality of the world— "by their fruits you shall know them." We can feel and observe that they are real. With Love at their core, these spirit reality elements of beauty, truth, and goodness are the hidden pearls of great price within us. Because creation is in and all around us, we have a tendency to be oblivious to it because it is so obvious. We are like little children lost in the garden of the universe; therefore, we can take the cause of all creation for granted; we don't really think about it too much, it's just like the family we are born into.

"If man's personality can experience the universe, there is a divine mind and an actual personality somewhere concealed in that universe." [2]

This is not referring to some concept of a personality depicted as a stern, wise old man with a long white beard, reclining in his rocker up in the clouds who's going to smack you out if you do something wrong. We are quite capable of doing that to ourselves. No, this is a personality that is saturated with the highest essence of Love that we could possibly imagine.

CHAPTER 5

Embracing the Core of Spirit Realities

In Chapters 1 and 2 we identified the basic elements of our thinking and how they work using the example of the primitive man collecting firewood. In Chapter 3 we identified that our values are the directional drivers or motivators that guide our choices of action. We have identified that our value system becomes the natural value keystone of our foundational archway for thinking; it becomes our seat of our identity! In Chapter 4 we discovered from actual living experience that the highest value in the universe is the *goodness of love*; that the non-material emerging elements of truth, beauty and goodness can be guided and enhanced by the spirit reality of the goodness of love because this love is actually made up, and is all-embracing of truth, beauty, and goodness. In the following chapters I'm hoping to reveal how the goodness of love plays a crucial role in the emergence of sustainable finite realities.

When we seek for the enhanced truth of the spirit value of the goodness of love and willingly embrace and apply it, we possess the ability to view reality from a higher perspective. We can do this because our freewill combines the evolving values with the enhanced insights of revealed spirit values that emanate and flow from this love. It's up to us to discern the differences between our emerging human morals and those revealed values gleaned from our awareness of the goodness of love. Our minds have the ability to recognise the benefits of their practical combinations that go towards giving us new insights and greater ability to engage with the challenges of life. Having this ideal of love within us motivates us to find and embrace truth. If there is anything in the universe we could trust, it is this love. Because we can trust this love, we can have faith in the *truth* of this love to guide us to a greater sense and appreciation of reality.

To cherish and be inspired by the goodness of love is a value that can only be found and lived by a freewill personality.

By analysing the mechanisms of mind and by observing the habits and construction of evolution, and by acknowledging the highest of values, I am looking for insights or clues in the hope of finding answers to some very big questions. Questions like; if freewill personality is essential for us to experience and know for a certainty that true love plays a vital role in our human condition, then where does personality actually come from? Why do we have freewill? What's the meaning of it all? Is there a master plan in the universe? Are we a part of some kind of unfolding adventure in which we can participate?

It's only upon reflection by living through the very experience of this universe that we can understand to a fuller extent the realness of a greater reality. We get to know people and understand their attributes through our relationships with them. It's only through personal relationships that we can come to an enhanced realisation of spiritual realities that are the personal realities of the universe; the un-ending, eternal, immortal aspects of the spirit realities of the universe which are truly beautiful and good; realities that have been there forever waiting to be discovered. We search for them and identify with them; there are no strings attached and there is no coercion.

By observing the evolution of material life, we may try to build a case to see if we can confidently add this "core of love" to the keystone of our thinking foundation. Again, we can ask but what is the origin of this core of love? What is its relationship to finite material reality? Is there a first cause in the universe—a primary source and centre to all things and beings that has personality? Again, if nothing can come from nothing, then a first cause must, at the very least, be personal. Is this what we call God? I'm going to define this as a creative personality that is simply behind the unfoldment of the universe where we can explore and discover the motivational will that causes this creation.

Spring Has Emerged and Life Is Astir

We can observe a large oak tree and appreciate its majestic beauty and how it adds beauty and ambience to the landscape. We are aware of a feeling of awe at the sight of such a magnificent specimen of nature. We may also realize the awesome fact that it takes in carbon dioxide and replenishes the air with oxygen so that creatures like us can live. We are not only stirred by its majestic beauty, but we also understand the role it plays and by so doing gives us a greater appreciation of its value.

Mother Earth provides us with all our basic needs; she sustains us and ministers to us by providing all the resources we need to engage creatively with reality. We naturally tend to give ourselves credit for the advancement of civilisation, and that's fine because we're the ones who have made the decisions and put in all the effort and hard yards, but rational thought also dictates that if our own personality and freewill is behind all that we create, so too is it reasonable to contemplate the simple idea of a personality behind the creation of the universe that is unified in spiritual realities. This first great source and centre to all things and beings is a great personality, one we can't fully comprehend or observe from our distant, lowly evolutionary position on the frontiers of time and space—our starting point of existence within finite reality. There's so much we don't know; all we can do is work with what we do know and keep searching and exploring the universe and our inner life for more understanding.

The endowment of our mind is also a living ministry to us because the phenomenon of intelligent mind is what we creatively use as we engage with the material world. On a higher level within us we can observe that the goodness of love continually ministers to us attempting to guide us onwards and upwards. This everlasting gift of ministry to our minds is the very essence of the Spirit's divine spiritual character, which is the universal gift to us—the spirit nucleus within. Therefore, because of this ministry of mind we can choose its leadings or not; our minds can be spiritualised and transformed by the recognition and willing adoption of the emerging values of Truth.

The first cause of all things and beings sets up and maintains a universal playing field of time-conditioned finite reality, then participates in a non-invasive way in creation. A crude analogy could be how our material brain automatically looks after many aspects of our material body such as keeping us breathing and pumping blood to the heart, the way our ears can hear, and our eyes can see. Behind the curtain of the beginnings of our material universe and its evolving life, we should postulate that the first cause to all things and beings is not entirely material. Our universe and its origin may contain much more than just the material theory of "the big bang." Creation is personally motivated by a reasoned desire to create and share. Imagine a creative personality with mind that is separate to us but very aware and involved in the creation of the material body of time and space—even the entire universe. It all must have been created by a mind that is capable of nurturing, watering, and maintaining the evolution of our material reality, just like we can experience pleasure in creating, maintaining, and caring for our gardens in our backyards.

Evolution is designed to have a directive purpose. A mind that is capable of creating and setting up an evolutionary environment for life must be the one who's seat of personal identity is the goodness of love. Why would a creator with mind and personality choose to do this? You could answer this with another question; Why do parents create children and care for them? We could answer, so their children can grow to recognize and appreciate the realness of all their potentials and possibilities within a universe whose gardener lovingly nurtures an awareness in them so that they can actually participate in their own evolving reality, and even participate in a higher reality when wedded to spiritual realities such as "love is the desire to do good to others." *[2]* Sharing is Godlike.

I sometimes think that the concept of embracing the emerging spirit realities of beauty, truth, and goodness is a bit like the three Musketeers pledging their allegiance to one another—"all for one and one for all". The first Musketeer of Truth is coherent, the second Musketeer of Beauty is attractive, and the third Musketeer of Goodness is stabilizing. They are all of equal value to one another. We discover their value in relation to our evolving understanding of things, meanings, and values, lifting us up and out of chaos through a personal metamorphosis that expands and transforms our minds, gathering us in, and drawing us towards the spiritual nucleus of the entire universe of time and space.

If the reality we create does not become coherent, attractive, and stabilising it is not a sustainable reality.

Differing Lenses of Perception

"Factual mediation" is one valued process of thinking for personal problem solving. By this I mean honestly laying out the facts of a given situation in our mind so we can ponder and analyse them truthfully and objectively. However, there are many other ways of thinking such as, when we are trying to work out how material things work, we need to focus just on the material aspects of reality. When astronomers and astrophysicists try to work out the age and beginning of our universe they just focus on the material—the mechanics of the observable universe—and they only "view" it and think about it from this material perspective. In doing this they tend to put aside any personal views and just consider the facts as they see them. From all this observation, they come up with what seems to them to be, a very plausible theory for the beginning of the physical universe. According to the standard Big Bang model theory, the universe was born during a period of inflation that began about 13.8 billion years ago. Then, like a rapidly expanding balloon, it grew from a size smaller than an electron to nearly its current size within a tiny fraction of a second. Attempting to figure out how our universe was born is an incredibly complex thing to try to work out, and all due credit to them in their ongoing efforts. However, it's a bit like being inside an egg trying to work out how an egg actually looks on the outside. They have been using the scientific method from within the egg! We must remember it is only a theory based on our current known material facts, and we must remember that the scientists are not viewing the universe from any personal philosophic perspective, they are simply viewing what they can understand so far, regarding the mechanics of the material universe.

We can also view the universe from a personal experiential perspective. By doing this we have the advantage of knowing the already discovered facts of the material universe while also being able

CHAPTER 5

to observe and philosophically analyse the other aspects of reality emerging from within us. While there are realities derived from the material world there are also the non-tangible realities emerging from personal experience that are just as real. We can observe and analyse these realities of meanings and values from our actual experience of living.

Let's see if it's possible to create an alternative theory of a first cause of reality using the same method of observation and analysis, except from the perspective of living, breathing, and thinking individuals. We can live with the Big Bang theory for now knowing that it may be expanded upon, or even completely changed as more scientific discoveries are made. However, add to the mix the discoveries found in our inner lives—those elements of beauty, truth, and goodness found through our ongoing personal experiences—and we may realise and come to appreciate that these spirit values can never be exhausted because at their core is Love which is felt to be timeless and limitless!

Even in the far distant future there may come a time when we have accumulated and exhausted our discovery of all the basic and spiritual elements within the known finite universe of experience, but this may not be an end in and of itself. We may have simply obtained a new foundation to stand upon to view an enhanced horizon of yet another new beginning of adventure and discovery. From the position of completion of experience and understanding of finite reality there is the real possibility that we will have evolved and obtained an experiential ability as individuals to continue to discover greater depths of beauty, truth, and goodness on higher and higher levels. Because these elements contain at their core the eternal goodness of love, they must be related to the first cause. We may understand that our insights of them are conditioned by time, but within the emerging realities of an individual, meaningful growth and understanding is always reaching towards something. We can't grow towards nothingness; that 'something' we grow towards must be **Truth**. There will always lie before us greater truths to be discovered, and greater challenges and adventures to experience.

In the words of Albert Einstein:

"I am not an Atheist. I do not know if I can define myself as a Pantheist. The problem involved is too vast for our limited minds. May I not reply with a parable? The human mind, no matter how highly trained, cannot grasp the universe. **We are in the position of a little child, entering a huge library whose walls are covered to the ceiling with books in many different tongues. The child knows that someone must have written those books.** It does not know who or how. It does not understand the languages in which they are written. The child notes a definite plan in the arrangement of the books, a mysterious order, which it does not comprehend, but only dimly suspects. That, it seems to me, is the attitude of the human mind, even the greatest and most cultured, toward God."

(Emphasis added.) [1] – *Albert Einstein*

So, with this as my premise I think the abode of the first cause of reality must contain within it the master blueprints of all creation while at the same time being the eternal centre of the material universe. This will forever be because its attributes that make up its characteristics and residence are all eternal realities. It is the spiritual nucleus of creativity, and it is this mind of creativity who created the mechanism for the creation of time and space. It innately functions on a level of absolute perfection. It is inherently good, beautiful, and true—the thought, the expression, and the act of this triune unity emanates from the nature and character of the personality which has eternal attributes of the goodness of love.

CHAPTER 5

The first cause is, by definition, the epicentre of the creation of our reality where the true elements of beauty, truth, and goodness emerge as they are discovered by us. The core of these spirit realities is revealed to be love to personalities and this love, along with the realities belonging to this love, are in existence before the finite realities of things, meanings and values expand, evolve, and grow. They are in existence before they can be discovered and understood from a finite, time-space perspective by our personal experiences. We, as individuals have the capacity to identify with them and distinguish their value because of their distinct qualities.

This theory of the first cause—the foundation of finite universe reality—lies behind and before any material theory such as the Big Bang. Our new and expanded theory rings true when viewed through the personal lens of perception of what makes up all the possible values that can be discovered and discerned in our reality. This experience should prove to the individual that the first cause is not material. The material universe and life within it may have a beginning and an ending, but the universal values of the realness of beauty, truth, and goodness originating in the core of love are endless and eternal; their origins are not created simultaneously within time and space. Their origin, while participating in time and space, lies outside the creation of time and space. Time is separated from the eternal so that personality within space and time can grow towards a more lasting and true reality. The material realities of things, meanings, and values are the foundations on which we stand to view, experience, and embrace the emerging spirit realities of the goodness of love contained within ourselves.

This concept can only be viewed from a personal perspective. We who come into existence within this evolving universe can, through mind, grow a new substance of reality by combining our discoveries of the values contained both in the basic elements and the values of their spirit counterparts of truth, beauty, and goodness. In this way we can become conscious of a new substance that results from the relationship of these emerging components of reality to one another. Our personal "golden value keystone"—our actual seat of identity—is transferrable to this new stable growing substance of reality—the evolution of our **soul** that can survive beyond our physical lives! (More on this later.)

This personal view of our individual relationships with reality and the universe does not discredit or invalidate the efforts of people like the scientists who are searching for the truth about material facts. We must consider these material aspects while also being aware of the truths gleaned from viewing and analysing the universe from the personal subjective point of view. Sharing our personal points of view with others about the origins of reality should be a rewarding experience because, quite often, the variety of personal viewpoints are not necessarily in conflict with one another.

Let's say that science looks for the truth in material things (facts); philosophy considers ideas about the facts and searches for beauty when attempting to weigh up how ideal their meanings and values are as they would play out in terms of practical utility; personal religion (spirituality) attempts to discover the ultimate goodness in values and attempts to explore their source of origin. These three views of differing realities (science, philosophy, and personal religion) should not conflict with one another as they are all required when we consider our foundational understanding of the basic elements. If all three pillars of such viewpoints are not accounted for then something is either disregarded, missing, or misinterpreted, which inhibits their unified relationship to one another, hence distorting the truth of the matter. We need the balance of all three to get a better sense of the wholeness of reality. In the creative realm of thinking, science, philosophy, and religion need not be divorced from one another in their individual pursuits for truth. After all, a greater appreciation of reality and a quest for truth are the goals of all three.

One Might Ask the Question

How many times do you hear questions and comments along these lines: If there's a God, why does he allow bad things to happen? If there's a God who's perfect and embodies all the goodness of love, then why are we and our world so imperfect? There can't be a God because if there was why would he create a world that contains so much suffering and evil? Why is there so much disease, pain and death? Why do we continually fight and destroy each other? Why and how could a God of love even think of creating an environment like this?

Let's think a little more deeply about this. We start out devoid of experience therefore cannot be instantly wise—we must learn as we grow. If we and our world were without error, how would we exercise our freewill to choose between right and wrong? A child might cry out against the injustices inflicted upon them by their wise and loving parents, but as they grow into adulthood, they carry no burden of resentment in their mature recollections that are based on understanding.

We know there is a natural law in nature—indeed in the universe—that we call "cause and effect". We know we are freewill creatures, therefore everything we do and say (cause) has consequences (effect). We, and those around us must live with the consequences of the freewill choices of others. We don't fully understand and grasp all the circumstances of our situation. But let's pause and consider the reality of our existence. We know we are born imperfect, and we know we are not all-knowing and wise; we don't always consider the consequences of our actions that inversely affect us physically, mentally, and intellectually both individually and collectively—we are a part of nature, and nature is not perfect. By observing the habits of nature, we see glimpses and patterns of perfection; while it can be beautiful and awe-inspiring it can also be brutal and cruel. We are vulnerable.

For creatures like us who are imperfect, let's imagine that our environment was created perfect—there was nothing to rip us apart or freeze us to death, no contrast of good and evil. How would we develop and grow? There would be no necessity to be motivated to make ourselves and our surroundings better. There would be no experiential understanding of truth, beauty, or goodness. There would be great limitations on our freewill choice. There would be no genuine appreciation of things without any contrasts to better our lot in life. There would be no creative striving towards perfection, there would be no discovery, nothing earned, no sense of satisfaction. We would just stay imperfect in a perfect environment; we would probably find that we would quickly destroy ourselves and no longer exist!

Our moral will is always bothered by the existence of evil and sin in our world. On one hand we deny the existence of an all-wise God because of this and on the other hand we readily blame God for allowing it to happen. It is hard for us to understand that the potential of evil and sin are inevitable for us to be truly free.

> "The uncertainties of life and the vicissitudes of existence do not in any manner contradict the concept of the universal sovereignty of God. All evolutionary creature life is beset by certain inevitabilities.

Consider the following:

> 1. Is *courage* — strength of character — desirable? Then must man be reared in an environment which necessitates grappling with hardships and reacting to disappointments.

> 2. Is *altruism* — service of one's fellows — desirable? Then must life experience provide for encountering situations of social inequality.

3. Is *hope* — the grandeur of trust — desirable? Then human existence must constantly be confronted with insecurities and recurrent uncertainties.

4. Is *faith* — the supreme assertion of human thought — desirable? Then must the mind of man find itself in that troublesome predicament where it ever knows less than it can believe.

5. Is the *love of truth* and the willingness to go wherever it leads, desirable? Then must man grow up in a world where error is present and falsehood always possible.

6. Is *idealism* — the approaching concept of the divine — desirable? Then must man struggle in an environment of relative goodness and beauty, surroundings stimulative of the irrepressible reach for better things.

7. Is *loyalty* — devotion to highest duty — desirable? Then must man carry on amid the possibilities of betrayal and desertion. The valor of devotion to duty consists in the implied danger of default.

8. Is *unselfishness* — the spirit of self-forgetfulness — desirable? Then must mortal man live face to face with the incessant clamoring of an inescapable self for recognition and honor. Man could not dynamically choose the divine life if there were no self-life to forsake. Man could never lay saving hold on righteousness if there were no potential evil to exalt and differentiate the good by contrast.

9. Is *pleasure* — the satisfaction of happiness — desirable? Then must man live in a world where the alternative of pain and the likelihood of suffering are ever-present experiential possibilities." [2]

Where is God?

In observing the laws of matter—the material universe and the existence of life—it seems that God is to a degree personally separated from being embedded in finite reality which virtually renders the actual personality of God invisible. We can see glimpses of the methods and habits of God by the contemplation and understanding of the wonder and awe of nature, but the person of God is not there! We simply cannot discover the actual person of God using the methods of scientific discovery in this finite universe.

The imperfect evolving finite aspect of matter and life does not, in and of itself reflect or fully represent the true nature and character of its creator, meaning something that is created becomes separate from the personality that created it, therefore it is not literally an acting part of the creator's personality. When the first person created the wheel, he or she was unable to control everything we did with that wheel afterwards. This is one of the innate laws of creativity so by this mere fact that finite reality is a creation and not an actual personality, God, its creator is personally separate to certain degrees from the function of its laws of cause and effect within this creation.

While the personality of God may uphold and direct the many fundamental laws of Creation, God also seems to have delegated creative responsibility to the living freewill creatures inhabiting this vast creation. For example, by falling over and breaking your leg that swells and becomes infected as you painfully hobble through the African jungle and come face to face with a hungry tiger confirms the fact that a God of love is not a personal participant. Once established, nature takes its course.

I think it's a worthwhile exercise to attempt to unpack all of this, to take a closer look at the big picture of finite reality. The intellectual tools we need are all there. In everything we see, we find we can call on the basic elements of reality to process and make decisions. These elements are embedded in the universe for us to discover and we have been given free will to do as we please. A way for us has been created within creation itself. We are simply living—we are walking around relatively freely in the creation of the mind of God.

So, where do we search for the *will* of God? Where do we search for the personality of God that is behind this creation we find ourselves in? Think about the part and the whole where we are the "parts" and all of creation is the "whole". It's hard for the part to understand or grasp the totality and purpose of the whole, let alone the will of its creator. Where can the part find a personal connection with the creator of the whole that can be grasped and related to? I believe that the greatness of God has amazingly and personally bridged this gap by giving us a fragment of divinity to indwell us. This is the parental endeavor by God to personally attempt to go into a partnership with us—to personally participate in, and be aware of our experiences, and to guide us in our creative endeavors all the while respecting the freewill of the individual which is paramount. The individual must choose to follow this guidance. There is no coercion on God's part.

Our directive power of choice is driven by our motivations, and motivations are energized by our personal value systems. When all is said and done it is our values that matter.

In the unfolding of the evolving universe the ingredient of choice—the creative potentials of a freewill life—determines the quality, meaning and purpose—the actuality, of the stage on which we exist and live out our lives. Everyone to some degree suffers the consequences of the choices of others; our choices can potentially affect everyone else. From our family and friends to our community, society and beyond, the more power of choice a person has, the greater the responsibility and effect they have on a greater number of people.

Brain Capacity and the "God Spot"

Scientists searching for a 'God spot' in the brain have recently found that there is not just one spot, as previously thought, but multiple spots that shows activity when people concentrate on religious and moral matters. Here are a few excerpts from some published articles from the University of Missouri Columbia (2012) on the subject.

"A study of 40 participants, including Christians, Muslims, Jews and Buddhists, showed the same areas lit up when they were asked to ponder religious and moral problems. MRI scans revealed the regions that were activated are those used every day to interpret the feelings and intentions of other people. 'That suggests that religion is not a special case of a belief system but evolved along with other belief and social cognitive abilities,' said Jordan Grafman, a cognitive neuroscientist at the National Institute of Neurological Disorders and Stroke in Bethesda, Maryland. Scientists, philosophers, and theologians continue to argue about whether religious belief is a biological or a sociological phenomenon. Some evolutionary theorists believe a belief in a religious power may have helped our ancestors to survive great hardship compared to those with no such convictions. Others argue that it arises from the structure of the highly adaptable brain itself. In the latest study, published in the journal, Proceedings of the National Academy of Sciences, Professor Grafman and his colleagues asked three types of question, while performing brain scans. First, volunteers were asked to think about statements about whether God intervenes in the world, such as 'God's will guide my acts'.

"This activated the lateral frontal lobe regions of the brain, used by humans to empathise with each other. Finally, the participants were asked to contemplate abstract statements such

CHAPTER 5

as 'a resurrection will occur'. This time they tapped into the right inferior temporal gyrus, which we use to understand metaphorical meaning. In all three cases the neural activity in the subjects' brains corresponded to brain networks known to have nonreligious functions. 'There is nothing unique about religious belief in these brain structures,' Professor Grafman said. 'Religion doesn't have a 'God spot' as such, instead it's embedded in a whole range of other belief systems in the brain that we use every day.' The networks activated by religious beliefs overlap with those that mediate political beliefs and moral beliefs, he said. Dr Andrew Newberg, director of the Centre for Spirituality and the Mind at the University of Pennsylvania, told the New York Times that Dr Grafman's findings were in line with other research that has so far failed to find any specific structure in the brain that is dedicated to religious belief. 'Religion has so many different aspects that it would be very unlikely to find one spot in the brain where religion and God reside,' Dr Newberg said. But he was doubtful that brain scans like those taken by Dr Grafman could capture all of what religion is. **'There may be other elements that science is not capable of measuring,'** Dr Newberg said. Professor Johnstone's findings claim that even the mind of world-renowned atheist Richard Dawkins is stimulated in the same way as a Christian or Muslim when they experience their minds' version of spirituality. In addition, Johnstone measured the frequency of participants' religious practices, such as how often they attended church or listened to religious programs. He measured activity in the frontal lobe and found a correlation between increased activity in this part of the brain and increased participation in religious practices. The research indicated that there are all kinds of spiritual experiences that Christians might call closeness to God and atheists might call an awareness of themselves.

"'We have found a neuropsychological basis for spirituality, but it's not isolated to one specific area of the brain,' said Brick Johnstone, professor of health psychology in the School of Health Professions. 'Spirituality is a much more dynamic concept that uses many parts of the brain.' 'Certain parts of the brain play more predominant roles, but they all work together to facilitate individuals' spiritual experiences.' He surveyed participants on characteristics of spirituality, such as how close they felt to a higher power and if they felt their lives were part of a divine plan. 'This is consistent with many religious texts that suggest people should concentrate on the well-being of others rather than on themselves.' Johnstone says the right side of the brain is associated with self-orientation, whereas the left side is associated with how individuals relate to others.

"While researchers have been focused on finding a 'God spot' in the brain, the new research suggests that **it might be better to focus on the neuropsychological questions of self-focus vs selfless focus.** As Prof. Johnstone explains, 'when the brain focuses less on the self (by decreased activity in the right lobe) it is by definition a moment of self-transcendence and can be understood as being connected to God or Nirvana. It is the sensation of feeling like you are part of a bigger thing.'"
(Emphasis added) [10]

All this makes sense to me in that the elements of beauty, truth, and goodness are involved across the entire range of thinking in relation to things, meanings, and values. The other interesting bit I gleaned from this new research is that it suggests it might be better to focus on the neuropsychological questions of concentrating on self as opposed to selfless focus and how individuals relate to themselves and others.

CHAPTER 5

So, the capacity of the human brain is enormous and complex when compared to that of the lower end of living creatures such as insects and bugs whose brain capacities are so obviously tiny that they could be described as mechanical or machine like. For instance, blow flies take about two weeks to grow to adulthood and then they're "good to go" but their life spans are short. Humans sit at the top of the scale of life and take the longest to grow, develop, and mature. They are the ones that are most dependent on their parents and society for their early development. Mind possesses a huge reservoir of functionality; it can view, collect, coordinate, and differentiate at the same time as unifying reality on three levels. The first view of reality is the basic view; the innate function of mind as being aware of facts, ideas, and their relation. The second view is from the combined emerging realities of experience—the elements of our human ideas and ideals of truth, beauty, and goodness. The third and highest view is made up of the truths that flow from our spiritual nucleus within—the goodness of love. Compared to insects like the bugs and flies, while they are amazing in and of themselves, we are obviously streets ahead in relation to our capacity to function, perceive, and create.

This large capacity for functioning also makes our relationships with one another incredibly complex as every personality is so unique. You can usually have meaningful and satisfying conversations with thoughtful people, whether they be an atheist, an agnostic, or a believer in God, because thoughtful people realise that there are unsolved mysteries to life and the universe. Most of these thinking people are truthful, decent, and caring having accumulated a good set of morals, ethics, and noble values. They are usually open to exploring, discussing, and considering differing points of view because they are motivated by being inquisitive towards the discovery of truth.

On the other hand, there are what I call the "five-minute" atheists and the "five-minute" religionists. By that I mean ones who have adopted certain opinions without carefully scrutinising them and are closed-minded to opinions that are not the same as their own fixed viewpoints. When I get involved in a conversation with these kinds of people, I often get quite irritated and tend to walk away thinking, "that was a conversation I shouldn't have had." But the worst thing I can think of is to attempt engaging in a meaningful conversation with a fanatic. Fanaticism blinds one to truth and creates preconceived prejudices; it can also cause one to become cruel and disruptive. It's like trying to engage with people on the far extremes of the political divide who hold strong attachments to their respective ideologies. It can cause sensible people to feel like running a mile from these kinds of encounters. But the saddest thing I find in this regard, is the way people with fixed and extreme points of view can turn away those innocent and possibly naive kinds of people who have not yet made up their minds about some of the big questions in life. Such people can easily shy away from engaging and discussing differing opinions with others about the rational aspects of reality, or about politics and religion as they need to feel safe when considering and exploring these big issues with others. I find this sad because it is naturally healthy and rewarding for us to be interested in listening and engaging with others on these subjects.

Objective and Subjective Time

We view and analyse reality both objectively and subjectively. This is especially true regarding time. I remember as a kid when I used to go on holidays with the family for three weeks it seemed to last a very long time; it was like experiencing a slice out of eternity. Now as an adult, when I have three weeks off, the time just flies; as a matter of fact when you hit 50 you realise that your life here is pretty short

CHAPTER 5

because you are now sitting in a subjective position where inwardly you can view your life where you can easily see the beginnings as well as everything in-between, and because of your accumulation of experiences, you can almost see right through to the end. You soon come to think "man, life flies—where did the time go?" My concept of time is not as long and stretched out as I once perceived it to be and because of this I am actually capable of doing a lot more in a day than I used to as a young person. When you are young time appears to be a continuing succession of events but as we accumulate more experience and memories, we tend to view time more subjectively in its wholeness; our sense of subjective time grows a timeless aspect to it where we can recall anything about our life instantaneously. At the same time, we become more acutely aware of the reality of objective time, but we don't seem to be so attached to it. It's a hard thing to explain but it's like we are growing out of time. It's our bodies wearing out that slows us down. You know that you're getting old when you have more memories behind you than you'll have ahead of you!

CHAPTER 6

Locating the Origin of Love—a Family Affair

My grandfather on my dad's side of the family was born in Marlow England in 1886. When the First World War broke out in 1914, he and his brother enlisted in the army. My grandfather was shot in the leg in one of their last charges on the German lines but despite that, both brothers managed to survive the muddy trenches of Flanders. After the war they received a Solders' Settlement Land Grant of 60 Acres in Australia, so they migrated there in 1920. Unfortunately, my grandfather's brother died six months later from pneumonia (which I suspect may have been the Spanish flu.) My grandfather established a dairy farm after clearing his plot of land. My dad was born on that farm in 1923. Then came 1930 when so many livelihoods began to fall over and shut down because of the Great Depression which hit Australia hard. My grandfather walked off his farm and the bank got the lot. Fortunately, he managed to secure work as a gardener on a huge sheep station called "Chatsworth House." He was supplied with a workers' cottage for his family and his wife secured work as a maid serving in the large house. My grandfather was in charge of the vegetable gardens and livestock that supplied the house and the large workforce with food. My dad had the good fortune of growing up on this 22,000-acre property of beautiful rolling hills with creeks and rivers as his backyard.

In 1939 the dark clouds of the doings of man came down with a heavy blow on our world once again; the Second World War broke out across Europe. In 1941, my dad applied to join the air force just after he'd celebrated his 18th birthday. He was accepted because they told him he had 20-20 vision and had obtained excellent marks in mathematics, physics, and geometry. So, off he went to South Australia for two months of intense training in navigation and it was here where he flew his first plane, a Tiger Moth biplane. After this initial training they divided the recruits into three groups; one group would train as bomber pilots, another as navigators, and the other fighter pilots. Dad was to become one of the fighter pilots and they were all to be trained in Canada. With a handful of other Australians, he headed off to Canada on board "The Orchidies", a passenger ship which departed from South Australia sailing across the Pacific, through the Panama Canal then up to the east coast of America to Montreal. After six months of training and flying Harvard planes he finally got his wings. He had one week off in New York then onto a passenger ship that joined a supply convoy escorted by battle ships to England. At that time, the crossing of the Atlantic in those supply convoys was a perilous journey as they were constantly under attack from German submarines (U-boats), nonetheless the convoy made it through and birthed in Liverpool on Christmas day 1942. The next day he was assigned to Montford airfield in Wales, and it was here he first laid eyes on a Spitfire. He trained for one week on Spitfires along with five others and then joined Squadron 64 at Gravesend airfield.

CHAPTER 6

Johnny Plagis & Frank Swadling *[11]*

The royal air force was devastated after the decisive Battle of Britain where so many pilots were tragically lost. In 1942 the English were still in desperate need of new pilots, so the refurbished Squadron 64 was made up of Poles, Canadians, French, Australians and New Zealanders. Because of the odd assortment of nationalities, Squadron 64 was nick named "The Odd Bods." Its Squadron leader was a Greek from Rhodesia who became a Spitfire Ace after fighting off the Luftwaffe in the air battle protecting the Rock of Gibraltar. His name was Jonny Plagis, just 24 years old, and he took dad under his wing. Within a few weeks dad was chosen to protect the Squadron leader in dog fights with the Luftwaffe because of his sharp vision and quick reflexes. At 19, Dad was the youngest among the pilots. Throughout this tour of duty with Squadron 64 the "Odd Bods" escorted bombers over Germany and attacked air force bases in Europe. They also completed numerous night raids off the Norwegian coast attacking German shipping supply lines, particularly focusing on oil containers. They executed these raids on clear full moon nights, flying just 20 feet above the sea to avoid being detected by German radar. These were dangerous missions as they only had ten minutes of extra fuel. Dad told me, "When you got in a dog fight you were often on and off full throttle and you could see the fuel gage dropping. Sometimes it was really tricky as you didn't want to run out of fuel and ditch in the winter Atlantic Ocean. We were told you only had about ten minutes before you froze to death in the icy sea." Squadron 64 also took part in the costly fighter sweeps over northern France that were designed to wear down the Luftwaffe. In 1944, after his tour in England, he was commissioned back to Australia where he was sent off for another tour at Milne Bay in Papua New Guinea fighting the Japanese until the end of the war in 1945.

My dad never talked about his war experiences until he was in his 80's. I remember one story he told me after I had been probing him with lots of questions. It was about a German weather plane that they were trying to shoot down over England. This plane flew at 30-35 thousand feet over England and was collecting weather information to help with the German air raids. Dad had two goes at trying to blast this thing out of the air. In the first attempt he got right behind it but couldn't fire his guns as they were completely frozen having jammed from the cold. On his second attempt he started firing at 25 thousand feet to keep the guns warm to prevent them from freezing up; he eventually managed to get behind this weather plane but by that time, he had run out of ammo. After the war Dad was in Brussels attending the international aviation conference as the Australian representative. It was here at this conference where the world governments had to decide what common language everyone should use for worldwide aviation. The French wanted French, but it was the Russian representative who aggressively persuaded everyone that it had to be English. After the conference Dad was having drinks with the German representative and asked him what he did during the war. It turned out that he was the pilot of that weather plane that Dad was trying to shoot down! They shook hands and became good friends and kept in touch over the years.

Why am I telling this story? I'm sure many of you reading this have similar family histories, but stories like these make us realise that life is a very fragile thing; life is so valued and is so precious, yet it's a miracle that many of us even exist! Our lives could end at the tick of a clock, anytime.

As I got to know my dad over the years it helped me to enlarge my circumscribed view. I was in a better position to look back on his life and generation more clearly. I had come to realise that he grew up on a sheep farm in an environment that at times, because of such a large number of different farm workers and shearers was, to say the least, somewhat rough and uncouth. This environment possibly contributed to the larrikin streak in him with a willingness for adventure. But I never observed a bone in my dad's body that was thoughtless or uncouth. I surmise that this is probably because his parents gave him lots of freedom as he was growing up which gave him the opportunity to observe a diverse array of the different character traits in human beings (i.e., the good, the bad and the ugly). But I think the great contributor to his good character that sustained him came from within his own family environment where there was a strong and united sense of ethics and morality—of being able to detect right from wrong. And I assume this sense of ethics and morality was absorbed into the foundations of the compass of his growing character, and from this contribution of family values, his selective choices went on to form his own sense of values which served him well.

I never got to know my Grandparents very well as there was such a separation of generations. They had already lived and experienced life while mine was just beginning. I was just entering young adulthood at the time they passed away; my Grandparents and their generation all seemed distant and irrelevant to me at the time. I felt that my generation (late 1960's) had moved on in leaps and bounds from the old-fashioned traditions and customs of past generations—we had "built-up steam" and were "entering unchartered waters". However, now, as I look back, I realise my Grandparents had inherited a cultural "compass" of many worthy qualities and values that were handed down and I have come to this realisation by reflecting upon what happened within my own family and its experiences. Many things that are not true get abandoned along the way and the things that are perceived to be true, get reused and continue to grow. When things are viewed through the experiential lens of a changing world, they tend to get corrected and updated. In this way it is the family that has the ability to be guided by the compass of truth; it is the family that collectively contributes to the direction and advancement of the cultural civilisation we inherit.

"Mating is purely an act of self-perpetuation associated with varying degrees of self-gratification; marriage, home building, is largely a matter of self-maintenance, and it implies the evolution of society. Society itself is the aggregated structure of family units. Individuals are very temporary as planetary factors — only families are continuing agencies in social evolution. **The family is the channel through which the river of culture and knowledge flows from one generation to another.**" *(Emphasis added)* [2]

It is through thinking about this that I have come to an understanding that we shouldn't judge the past, or even others by our own present value standards. We always need to look at the context of the person or the time placement of civilisation—the hows, whys, and wherefores of the reality of circumstances. By taking this into account I believe we can get a clearer understanding of the past by judging it by its own value standards because the context and reality of the present is very different from the context and circumstances of the past. We build on the truth; it will always remain as a truth, and we need to keep hold of this truth. The beauty of lasting truth is that it is very adaptive to the changing times—we should never ignore the truth. As the saying goes, "don't throw the baby out with the bathwater" but at the same time "don't put new wine into old wineskins".

The Enlarged Family—A Universe Affair

We evolved out of a warm saline soup, and we belong to a species that eventually became freewill, complex, and creative **persons**. As I've said before, the first cause behind the creation of all this evolution can't be anything less than what we have become. What we're now looking for is to extend this idea of family to include the universal first cause and to find our relationship to this first cause in the hope that we may enlighten our minds to recognise the actual origin of our highest value—the goodness of love. Experiencing the truth of this relationship has the potential to change our outlook forever.

We have already explored our ongoing personal evolving relationships by identifying the basic and emerging elements. We have experientially realised the value of love and the beneficial realities of truth, beauty, and goodness that flow from its core. We identified that this love is the highest value we can envision; when it all boils down, real love—high minded love—means more to us than anything else. Love is a value that is experienced only by being known, rather than by understanding a mere teaching or idea. It is a value that emanates from within a personality, and it is only shared and known by personalities. Now we are going to look at taking the next logical step and try to locate the **origin** of this powerful, all-pervasive kind of love to see if it's feasible for us as individuals to develop a relationship with the actual first cause of all this finite reality. This relationship will be an inner and personal experience for us, but the unique quality of this next level of relationship experience is that it will be the beginning of a relationship between two actual personalities; it will not be just our personal consciousness of things, meanings, and our growing awareness of teachings and ideas of values; it will not be simply a hypothetical philosophical concept; **rather it will be a growing experience as real as the relationships we have with our cherished family and friends.**

If the core of the first-cause personality is the actuality of this powerful and all-pervasive kind of love, it is only by developing a relationship, a connection with this personality that we will find the answers to the true meaning and the true value of our existence. Otherwise, we will forever remain a mystery to ourselves and simply look upon humans as a freaky evolutionary accident. We discover the source, and experience a greater reality of this new value and its integral elements, only through our inner experience and understanding of this relationship.

CHAPTER 6

There are great benefits to having a relationship with the first cause of creation. It's full of possibilities, and is definitely worth exploring because, although a relationship like this may seem a little daunting, or on the surface may sound quite ridiculous or impossible—definitely "out of my league" so to speak—here we are as personalities with the potential to interact with other personalities, and, as with all meaningful personality relationships, there are obviously personal aspects to it so that both of us can actually relate to and share with one another; and best of all, the love aspect between personalities can be experienced and shared. The personality of the first cause may even adapt to our reality in a similar way a parent does with a growing child. The creation and evolution of the universe is a family affair—a universal family affair; we are sons and daughters of the will of the creator.

Let's keep in mind that we already have experienced the water of beauty, truth and goodness flowing through the veins of our experiences. As we thirst for it, we go about living our lives. It's not what we actually are in any given moment, it is what we are striving for and slowly becoming day by day. We know that the emerging realities are not material and yet they are just as real to us as material things and are priceless—they are of more value than our material treasures. Some might argue that they are just imaginations and inventions of the mind, but the possibility of beautiful and meaningful repercussions can emerge and be created from them. But let's remember, we haven't resolved all the questions that surround the *origin* of our minds yet. I would prefer to consider the recognition of reality as being an *awareness* of mind, an *understanding* of mind through our *experiences* with these realities.

We have explored the idea that the cause of the basic and emerging elements emanates from love, and we have concluded that love could not be expressed, could not be shared, could not be bestowed—would not even exist—if it were not for personality and freewill. We have rationalised and concluded that the first cause cannot contain anything less than what we have observed and analysed as being real within our finite universe. We have concluded that everything in our existence cannot come from absolutely nothing. These elements we have recognised, and become aware of, would not originate from a mechanistic, material universe made up of only material matter. The elements of love could not emanate from anything purely material. Therefore, we can have a reasoned faith in the value of the goodness of love because this is not a blind faith; its very foundation is based on reason and personal experience.

So again, what if the core of creation was somewhere deep inside us and has been there right from the beginning? If we take on the idea that a fragment of the cause of creation lives within us as a "divine spark" then the idea of the outside already being inside—even though it may be a bit weird to grasp—is an idea worth unpacking, exploring, experiencing, and testing. As a child this concept wasn't foreign to me; it was "I and I" and we got along just fine.

Some things in our inner life are hard to see because all the components that make us persons function as one. As a child I was oblivious to the vital role my parents and my environment played regarding my experiences, welfare, and growth. Something so obvious is not readily recognised in the immature child, but even in the case of mature adults, when focussing on a given task, they can easily be oblivious to something highly obvious to others not focused on that task. A great example of this was found in an experiment that was undertaken where a video was made of a group of people playing with a ball and the viewers were instructed to count how many times the ball was passed between the players. While they were intent on counting the number of times the ball was passed a gorilla entered the room, stopped centre stage, thumped his chest, and then walked off but when the viewers were asked later if they saw the gorilla in the room, not one of them saw it because they were so intent on counting!

CHAPTER 6

Just because an awareness of our personal relationships within and towards the universe are not right there in full view of our conscious understanding, let's not abandon the idea of a *divine spark* or fragment of the core of creation as residing within us simply because we haven't spent enough time pondering or thinking deeply about it. We may not have consciously recognised its workings and benefits that have naturally flowed from all the components within us—all those things that have added to our depth of understanding, those things that have naturally contributed to the richness of our experiences, our thinking, and choices, those things that have quietly contributed to our conscience, our awareness, and our morals and values.

> "Science may be physical, but the mind of the truth-discerning scientist is at once supermaterial. Matter knows not truth, neither can it love mercy nor delight in spiritual realities. Moral convictions based on spiritual enlightenment and rooted in human experience are just as real and certain as mathematical deductions based on physical observations, but on another and higher level." [2]

If someone is willingly led by the spirit within, their fruits over time are naturally displayed in their lives. If a professed religionist judges another person's emerging spiritual worth as not being truly religious because they do not adhere to their beliefs and doctrinal criteria on what one should say and do to be saved, they are sadly missing the point! "By their fruits you shall know them." No wonder so many so called non-religious people feel indignant towards these types of unenlightened religionists! Many of us may be unaware of the contribution the goodness of love plays in our spiritual growth. For example, a young child is basically unconscious of the ongoing efforts of their parents towards their growth. You can't watch yourself grow so to speak; growth is something you understand in retrospect.

We experience, learn, and grow; we get a sense of satisfaction and achievement by sharing our lives with others, so we have learnt to place a very high value on our relationships. By sharing our inner life with the first cause of creation we also have this value-added personal relationship within us; a divine parental companion as we embark upon the challenge of our personal adventure of life within the universe.

> "Notwithstanding that God is an eternal power, a majestic presence, a transcendent ideal, and a glorious spirit, though he is all these and infinitely more, nonetheless, he is truly and everlastingly a perfect Creator personality, a person who can "know and be known," who can "love and be loved," and one who can befriend us…" [2]

I remember as a kid I had this loyal imaginary friend within (like an alter ego), who was always there as we went through the adventures of my vivid subjective imaginary play life. "Let's do this," I used to say to myself as I jumped up and ran down the hill, "we're doing this together." Me and my imaginary friend always had the courage and confidence to know what to do as we tore off into the wild unknown, confronting and surmounting the most difficult things in our objective world of reality. I spent hours immersed in these exciting and joyful imaginary adventures. Together we were undefeatable!

We need to examine this idea of an indwelling spark of divinity on a personal level. I must confess it's not going to be easy to test and fully understand a mystery like this one in our lives, but let's bear with it because I think we can build a reasonable and sensible case for its inclusion; one that's not overly complex. Let's assume that a part of this core of creation is centred deep inside us—so much so that our day-to-day function of material consciousness is not fully comprehending or accessing it in the material day-to-day workings of our mind. Our enlightened moment of realisation may not have yet occurred. It would be a faith adventure of acceptance, but this adventure would not be a blind faith-adventure; it would be based on intellectual reason and personal experience. We may not have recognised and fully understood this truth-gem yet nor placed it into our value keystone because our evolving human attributes make us incomplete—we're still growing and "a pint cannot hold a quart." However, within the finite realities of our existence, we are in the early stages of our career when analysing or looking for our relationship to certain mysterious realities. They cannot be forced into our memory mould; an element of time, freewill choosing, experience, and pondering is required for them to be recognised. But despite all this, an understanding of the concept of this truth-gem can happen now if we understand the simplicity of a great truth—and that great truth is that this gem is simply the "goodness of love", and we can freely choose to embrace our comprehension of it and place it into our value keystone.

Let's follow this line of thought a while longer; it may be the hidden gem concealed within that is missing and needs to be placed into the value hierarchy of our keystone. This goodness of love may be likened to a well that is filled with the infinity of the water of truth, a guiding gift from the universe placed inside us waiting to be discovered; a gift to assist us in our relationships with one another and the universe; a simple gift—an undiluted fragment of love—a timeless fragment consisting of the realities of the goodness of love.

Even though we may be unconscious of the contributions that the goodness of love plays in our growth, being unconscious of this fact doesn't matter. For example, as I said before a young child is basically unconscious of the efforts of its parents' contributions towards their growth. The fact of being unconscious of this fact is irrelevant if you are willing to be led; the outcomes are the same. Again, you can't watch yourself grow; growth is something you understand in retrospect.

Just as values are learnt and transmitted through the relationships of our earthly families, so too can there be a child-parent relationship between our emerging values and the maturity of the goodness of love.

CHAPTER 7

Personality, Conscience, and Spirit Realities

An Attempt to Define Personality

In the hope of avoiding possible confusion when following my thought streams, before moving on in the exploration of why these new elements are of value and how we can grow in our understanding of them and continue to incorporate them into our foundation for thinking, it may be helpful for me to define my understanding of Personality. In trying to define what personality is, I will attempt to do this by observing how it seems to work.

I think Personality has got to be up there and counted as the mystery of mysteries. I'm not going to pretend that this attempt at a definition is anything scientific or authoritative as I'm not an expert on the subject. Personality seems to be the pattern of our unique and individual existence. When all our components of body and mind are put together and are acting as one, it is our individual *personality* that saturates and unifies us. I can't quite nail it down, but I can observe a few of its characteristics—what it tends to do. It's what gives us our unique identity but because it is unifying our various components it's not actually an obvious component in and of itself. To use a crude analogy, it's a bit like a colour—you can't touch a colour, but you can touch something that has that colour painted on it. Take away the object and you don't see the colour on its own—they are inseparable. Everyone has a unique "colour" (figuratively speaking), and my colour is uniquely different to yours, it is the real *unchanging* part of us that continues to identify us throughout our lives. I don't believe our physical bodies accurately reflect our personalities. It takes an element of time for us to grow, and it takes time for us to get to know someone. For example, if someone has a bubbly predisposition, we might say they have a "bubbly personality" but as we know, someone can be gorgeous on the outside but very different on the inside. Observation has taught me that personality is a lot more than that. I believe it also takes an element of time for our personality to unify the experiential parts of our lives. Despite all our inherited tendencies that we receive from our ancestors, those underlying roots of our nature and character are not personality; personality can be observed as something separate from our inherited DNA. Whatever it actually is, it is totally unique for each person.

Personality is a mystery and can be likened to a gem; a precious gift that is bestowed on the physical "us" perhaps at birth. We can only observe the attributes of people's personalities by our relationships with them. Once we really get to know someone, even as they age and physically change, we can still recognize them because it is, for the most part, their personality that we recognise. Personality functions within our inherited genic tendances of nature and character, but it is also free of them; its freewill is separate so I think it must be indissolubly linked with freewill and must be at the very core of our being. It has the power to adapt to and change and improve our natural inherited habits and characteristics; it also has an innate power to transform, control, and unify all the constituent parts of our very being. It is our personality that makes the choices that determine our successes and failures and the rate of our evolutionary growth.

Personality is inherently that creative part of us. While certain animals are creative in that they can instinctively build things, for example beavers can build dams, spiders can spin webs, and birds can build nests etc., the creativity of human personality is something vastly different. Each of our personalities are unique and while our personalities have common attributes in that we all possess freewill and can be experientially aware and conscious, we can differ greatly in the choices we make and what to do with our creative abilities. We are able to discern truth and make ethical and moral decisions regarding how we act, and we consciously decide what we choose to create. Freewill creativity and being morally aware are observable attributes of personality that are distinctly different to the genetically inherited habits and capabilities of the minds of our animal cousins. It is quite easy to predict the behavioural habits of different animals but when it comes to humans it is utterly amazing what the creative personality of individuals can achieve; the possibilities are unpredictable. For us to be truly free and for freewill to function means we need to have the capacity to be aware of ethics, morality, and the meaning of truth and the value of things. Our personality can function by using more of mind than the animals because we have a greater capacity of receptivity to accommodate all the pre-requisites needed for freewill. The creative endowment of the uniqueness of our personality is the only explanation as to why we are so different to animals.

When we look within and around us, it is our personality that seems to be the only thing that's permanent in the presence of growth and change. There seems to be only two unchanging aspects within us—one is our personality, the other is the spiritual nucleus of Love. However, the relationship between the two of them is nothing but growth and change, yet somehow through this whole process of the growth through life, our identity—our personality remains changeless. Because our freewill is indissolubly linked to our personality, it's our personality that unifies all the parts that make up ourselves, regardless of whether those parts are incomplete, misaligned or even deranged. Our personality faithfully reflects all this by its innate tendency to unify, thus reflecting the realty of the totality of ourselves at any given time.

If you really think hard about yourself and others in relation to death, what would we naturally crave for in death? My answer to that is survival of self, survival of our personality. Personality remains a mystery. Regardless, here we are!

Primitive humans tended to personalise everything because they were personalities themselves. They did this simply because they literally lacked the experience of understanding things in relation to reality. They had not accumulated the knowledge and scientific understanding of all the facts of cause and effect of the material reality around them. They couldn't distinguish between this natural phenomenon of material reality and their evolving understanding of the personal values of personality. It is our personality that recognises values so if we did not have a personality, we would purely function on the animal level of existence. The beauty of all this has shown us that the evolving appreciation of values is indissolubly linked to personality. Without personality there would be no value element to be discovered or experienced and we would not be able to recognise and cherish goodness as a value.

> "The concept of truth might possibly be entertained apart from personality, the concept of beauty may exist without personality, but the concept of divine goodness is understandable only in relation to personality." [2]

CHAPTER 7

"Only a philosophy which recognizes the reality of personality—permanence in the presence of change—can be of moral value to man, can serve as a liaison between the theories of material science and spiritual religion." [2]

The Confusion Surrounding Conscience

There is a lot of confusion between spiritual values and conscience which can and does cause problems. Conscience is simply our own ethical and moral prompting of ourselves. Our conscience is derived from many sources; it can be comprised of components of values from our upbringing and influenced by the ethics, morals, and values of the mores of our surrounding culture coupled with our own personal standards of justness and fairness. Albeit it is the worthy foundation upon which we stand, but we must be aware that it is by no means perfect. My own experience has shown me that my conscience is what I feel or believe to be right, and it will let me know if I am doing something or thinking something that I feel, or know, is wrong. The wonderful thing about conscience is that it can correct itself; it's not set in stone; over time it can grow its moral and ethical fibre by being sensitive to truth. It is the essential foundation that provides us with a strong balanced character. It also seems to be very sensitive to criticism and sometimes makes us overly judgemental of others. **It is not the voice of God directing us. Also, it is not the wrath of God pointing the finger of guilt at us.** A guilty conscience is often you simply beating yourself up because you did something wrong or stupid. Also, there's nothing worse than being exposed to someone with an overly sanctimonious conscience and there's nothing more debilitating for someone to have an overly sensitive self-critical conscience.

Below are some nice little quotes about aspects of our conscience that I have found helpful in understanding what our conscience is, and what it is not, and how it operates.

"...conscience, untaught by experience and unaided by reason, never has been, and never can be, a safe and unerring guide to human conduct. Conscience is not a divine voice speaking to the human soul." [2]

"Growth is also predicated on the discovery of selfhood accompanied by self-criticism—conscience, for conscience is really the criticism of oneself by one's own value-habits, personal ideals." [2]

"The presence of goodness and evil in the world is in itself positive proof of the existence and reality of man's moral will, the personality, which thus identifies these values and is also able to choose between them." [2]

"Only a moral conscience can condemn the evils of national envy and racial jealousy." [2]

Below are some more quotes from one of the geniuses of our world in the field of the philosophy of living and in the practical application of *spirit values* in the living of one's life. When we separate Jesus' teachings by stripping away the theology and dogma that was built up around him, his depth of insight remains profound. I've included these quotes to illustrate the difference between "spirit values" and "conscience", because there is a lot of confusion between the two.

"... You are not to go hence in the proclamation of the kingdom, saying, 'it is here' or 'it is there,' for this kingdom of which you preach is God within you." [2 & 9]

"...Seek first the kingdom of God, and when you have found entrance thereto, all things needful shall be added to you." [2 & 9]

"...The faith of Jesus visualized all spirit values as being found in the kingdom of God; therefore he said, 'Seek first the kingdom of heaven.'" [2 & 9]

He wasn't talking about "conscience" he was talking about *all* spirit values that are comprised of the spirit reality aspects of beauty, truth, and goodness.

Spirit-Value Realities

Some may think that the spirit-value realities that flow and emerge into reality from the goodness of love—the ones that contribute to enhancing our ability to appreciate beauty, truth, and goodness—are just natural constructs of the human mind thereby denouncing any such thing as having spiritual value. Ok, but even if they are thought to be just constructs of mind, when material mind is sensitive towards them, when we become aware of them regardless of belief or understanding, we still acknowledge them. These constructs and discovery of emerging elements of value are not material but they are real nonetheless; through our consciousness of mind, we become aware of them by interacting with reality and people, and by reflecting on our experiences. They are essential emerging components of our reality. They are experienced and felt within the relationship of our person towards other persons and in our relationships towards our environment.

The natural constructs of mind innately work with its system of thinking regarding things, meanings, and values, and these qualities that we are dealing with are very real in our everyday lives. (Recall our working example of the thinking process of the primitive man collecting firewood.) Our consciousness can and does work in a similar way regarding the quality overlay of beauty, truth, and goodness. Consciousness, as an aspect of personality in action can perceive these realities in daily living. As persons, we perceive they are real and our perception of them can be enhanced by being sensitive towards truth; our freewill has the prerogative to accept, reject, or simply ignore them. The imbedded pattern of the evolution of life enables us to be receptive and responsive to all these emerging elements of reality. You see this displayed when you observe children enjoying playing together. You will often see how they create an enthusiastic willingness to cooperate; you can witness the early stages of their display of moral choices. The non-material domain within us is where our freewill operates, and within this domain can be added a spiritual element. The important thing to recognise and remember here is that the inclusion of these emerging elements greatly benefits our thinking processes and contributes to the quality of our foundation of thinking.

As we bumble along, participating in the unfolding of finite reality, we need to take a serious look at this idea of spiritual realities overlaying and infusing our rational framework of thinking. With their relationship added to our collection of things, meanings and values, our minds can grasp their relevance and importance. I see these emerging value realities as being an intrinsic, potentially directive influence that contributes to the wholeness of our reality. Once we recognise the natural driving forces of evolution within us, we should embrace them and not ignore them for, in a sense, they could be considered as "the will of the creator." Once understood, you could say that we've earned a learner's permit that allows us to participate in the spiritual quest for higher meanings in our lives. If there is validity to spirit realities and we don't personally recognise or accept that they are real contributing elements (ones that can enhance our perceptions if we integrate these higher aspects to our thinking) we would continue hobbling along with only one eye, one view to reality, failing to understand a large chunk of the truth that makes up the components of our very being, our purpose for existence, the direction of evolution, our very relationship to what is real. Without pursuing their "origin" life just becomes an endless "Groundhog Day" for civilisations, endlessly confronting the same problems.

> "Spirituality enhances the ability to discover beauty in things, recognize truth in meanings, and discover goodness in values. Spiritual development is determined by capacity therefore and is directly proportional to the elimination of the selfish qualities of love." [2]

Note that the above quote says, "Spirituality *enhances* the ability…" it doesn't say that spirituality literally *gives* you the ability; it is up to us to put forth intelligent efforts of engagement with all the elements as we confront the choices that reality continually throws at us.

It's Not Just All About Matter and Energy

> "Mathematics, material science, is indispensable to the intelligent discussion of the material aspects of the universe, but such knowledge is not necessarily a part of the higher realization of truth or of the personal appreciation of spiritual realities. Not only in the realms of life but even in the world of physical energy, the sum of two or more things is very often something more than, or something different from, the predictable additive consequences of such unions. The entire science of mathematics, the whole domain of philosophy, the highest physics or chemistry, could not predict or know that the union of two gaseous hydrogen atoms with one gaseous oxygen

atom would result in a new and qualitatively superadditive substance—liquid water. The understanding knowledge of this one physiochemical phenomenon should have prevented the development of materialistic philosophy and mechanistic cosmology.

"Technical analysis does not reveal what a person or a thing can do. For example: Water is used effectively to extinguish fire. That water will put out fire is a fact of everyday experience, but no analysis of water could ever be made to disclose such a property. Analysis determines that water is composed of hydrogen and oxygen; a further study of these elements discloses that oxygen is the real supporter of combustion, and that hydrogen will itself freely burn." [2]

I really like this analysis of the elements of water which I also touched on earlier. I think it's a great analogy for the illustration of what might happen when we combine all the elements we have now identified, that go towards our thinking processes. When we add to our accumulated understanding of things, meanings, and values, the enhanced insights derived from the emerging elements of beauty, truth, and goodness, we have the potential to create a new growing substance to our thinking process that changes the value keystone of our foundation for thinking. This combination mixed and functioning within our minds produces an alchemy of elements that create a new and greater substance within the keystone of our thinking and our seat of identity which can choose to sit within this "golden value keystone".

"In science the human self observes the material world; philosophy is the observation of this observation of the material world; religion, true spiritual experience, is the experiential realization of the cosmic reality of the observation of the observation of all this relative synthesis of the energy materials of time and space. To build a philosophy of the universe on an exclusive materialism is to ignore the fact that all things material are initially conceived as real in the experience of human consciousness. The observer cannot be the thing observed; evaluation demands some degree of transcendence of the thing which is evaluated." [2]

CHAPTER 8

Natural Blockers to the Goodness of Love

The way I see it is that the main blocker to fully embracing the goodness of love are our **selfish qualities of love**. Ouch! As we all should know, the natural human tendencies towards the selfish qualities of love, when they involve personal relationships, can cause our lives to become quite messy and irritating not just to ourselves but also to those around us; our thoughtlessness towards others plays into its hand—the selfish quality of love is always clamouring for attention which causes us to place emphasis on ourselves. Our animalistic tendencies are a part of our innate material makeup. These tendencies, and our inability to master ourselves, when left unchecked can lead to undesirable—even dire—consequences. By knowing ourselves and by being aware of these propensities helps us to become more aware of the effect our actions have on others.

Selfishness can create its own hell where we can torment ourselves and others. But let's not beat ourselves up too much about this; a little understanding coupled with the support of our ongoing attempts at self-mastery go a long way. A simple natural antidote to this tendency towards the "selfish qualities of love" is to remind ourselves to focus on the "goodness of love" which is forever at hand within ourselves, and to consider the integrity and sanctity of every other personality. The goodness of love has incredible attributes we should all thirst for; it holds within it the fruits that yield for example; forgiving tolerance, loving service, unselfish devotion, sincere fairness, enlightened honesty, confiding trust, courageous loyalty, undying hope, and enduring peace.

If it is true that the ideal of the emerging elements of beauty, truth, and goodness are elements driven and guided by the goodness of love, how would we prove it? It certainly can't be proved by scientific methods, but then scientific methods are not designed for and are not meant to be used and applied in attempting to prove things that are not entirely in the material realm. Don't let the façade of scientific materialism render God invisible. In my mind there is only one way to prove the spiritual values of Love and that is through personal experience which must be known and felt to be true, then to be lived—and they must be lived to be seen. "Truth is coherent, beauty attractive, goodness stabilizing." [2] These are values that are real to *people*. They are not real to machines! These are realities that are just as real to a thinking person as that chair you may be sitting on. We should spend some time sincerely thinking about this. You know what you know, and only *you* know what you feel and know to be true and good. We should also think about why and how we come to know they are personally true! The water of beauty, truth, and goodness flows through our experiences, and if a "lover" did not reside within us, we may not even feel the truth of their entrance into our hearts! Once again:

CHAPTER 8

"Spirituality enhances the ability to discover beauty in things, recognize truth in meanings, and discover goodness in values. Spiritual development is determined by capacity therefore and is directly proportional to the elimination of the selfish qualities of love." [2]

We're born into life with a kind of mindal software that's loaded with predispositions. We are packaged with the incredible living instrument of mind, which we operate within the material neuron circuitry of our brains. Through accumulated experiences and growth, we can realize that by simply using the 'lite' version of our software in our value keystone—meaning we are just focussing on material reality—perception within individuals and civilisation has limited ability to process everything correctly. As we develop, grow, and become more complex, there's not enough to get answers to all the important questions we're confronted with about the mysteries of life; there's just not enough to fully sustain us in the forward momentum of advancing civilisation. Therefore, we need to upgrade and click on the premium version of the software within us—the one that has all the bells and whistles and added pulldowns of our emerging understandings of beauty, truth, and goodness, the origins of which flow directly from the goodness of love within us. It is this goodness that we simply need to place into our golden value keystone to stimulate us to search for and to feel and consider—to test out these emerging realities by willingly infusing and adopting them into our relationships with others. In so doing we can attach ourselves to them and climb up another rung on the Finite Ladder. Just as science continues to search material reality for facts, we too should be just as keen to investigate the workings of our minds and discover the potential possibilities of accessing the resources that flow from this beautiful gift of the goodness of love. Sometimes the most obvious things are right there in front of us, and because they are so simple and obvious, we just don't see them.

Even on the material level there have been some amazing discoveries and inventions that are so simple you have to wonder why it took us so long to discover or invent them. One that comes to mind is the S-bend in plumbing. For thousands of years humanity has put up with the stench of human waste; of urine and faeces from the plumbing systems in towns and cities by letting the odours of sewerage waft back up the drains and pipes. It wasn't until 1775 when an S-shaped trap, known as an S-bend was invented by Alexander Cumming. This became the missing ingredient to the success of the flushing toilet and, with it came public sanitation as we know it. Flushing toilets had previously floundered on the problem of smell coming back through the pipe that connects the toilet to the sewer. Cummings' solution was simplicity itself: bend the pipe. Water settles in the dip, stopping smells coming up; flushing the toilet replenishes the water! I'm amazed that for so long not one individual out of a vast sea of humanity had ever thought of this. (Later on, the modern flushing toilet was invented by Mr. Crapper—and amusingly, his name was shortened and now lives on!) Maybe things need to get so bad that it literally forces us into thinking about solutions.

Why Do Civilisations Fall?

We are tied to reality by the natural forces of cause and effect; it does what it does, and it pushes us either forward or over the edge. Let's take a brief look at the history of just a few of our civilisations like Egypt, Greece, and Rome and ask, what on earth happened to them? They lasted so long and then disintegrated—they are no more. As they grew, they became more complex, and when they reached a certain point of sophistication and complexity there began a slow decline before their civilisations collapsed. So we pick ourselves up, sift through the ruins, collect the remnants, and start building the next civilisation. We must ask the questions: was there anything lacking in our predecessors' visions? What went wrong? What did they overlook? Or is this just the harsh reality of the natural process of cause and effect that we need to go through to learn the hard lessons of attempting to develop sustainable cultures, societies, and politics? We have freewill and as time unfolds, I suspect we need to incorporate spirit realities into our thinking processes to unify and sustain our forward thrust in evolution. Because personality is creative, we are a different kettle of fish to the abundant plant and animal life that share our world.

"A lasting social system without a morality predicated on spiritual realities can no more be maintained than could the solar system without gravity." [2]

We are now standing in our current timeline of civilisation, and we can see that we are in a period of transition and rapid change—our civilisation has become specialised and complex. If we don't want to end up like ancient Greece and Rome, we should be proactive rather than reactive and we should carefully examine history and attempt to identify the reasons for the apathy that precedes the disruption that places its hand on the reset button of civilisation.

> "The social ship has steamed out of the sheltered bays of established tradition and has begun its cruise upon the high seas of evolutionary destiny; and the soul of man, as never before in the world's history, needs carefully to scrutinize its charts of morality and painstakingly to observe the compass of religious guidance. The paramount mission of religion as a social influence is to stabilize the ideals of mankind during these dangerous times of transition from one phase of civilization to another, from one level of culture to another." [2]

Religious beliefs and rituals have been found in every society studied by anthropologists. This implies that the religious/spiritual experience is a universal characteristic of human nature just like the ability to see in colour. Religion could not have evolved and affected the lives of most of the world's human inhabitants if it had not helped them in some way to solve the problems of surviving adversity and successfully raising children who would propagate their supernatural belief systems down through the generations. So it makes sense that the inner workings of the brain (or mind) are inherently geared for those particular response mechanisms that result in religious experiences. Indeed, an evolutionary perspective on religion implies that humans are inherently susceptible to religious views.

"Man evolved through the superstitions of mana, magic, nature worship, spirit fear, and animal worship to the various ceremonials whereby the religious attitude of the individual became the group reactions of the clan. And then these ceremonies became focalized and crystallized into tribal beliefs, and eventually these fears and faiths became personalized into gods. But in all of this religious evolution the moral element was never wholly absent. The impulse of the God within man was always potent. And these powerful influences—one human and the other divine—insured the survival of religion throughout the vicissitudes of the ages and that notwithstanding it was so often threatened with extinction by a thousand subversive tendencies and hostile antagonisms." [2]

What we collectively hold as known values creates cohesiveness within our societies. The depth of reality of the goodness of these values faithfully reflects the degree of the actual quality of our societies.

CHAPTER 9

Transferring Our Seat of Identity

I think it's reasonable and quite exciting to conjecture that the emerging spirit elements can become actual possessions of freewill personalities like us and can have a flow on effect in our contributions to society and civilisation. I'm all up for looking into becoming more than I am. I can already rationalise and see the benefits these spirit realities would give us, not the least of which is a greater opportunity to participate and endure in the plan and outcomes of finite creation.

By choosing to apply our rational material thinking to the contemplation and consideration of spiritual realities—such as looking for the beauty content in all things and of finding insights into the truth of meanings, as well as deciding if there is a genuine truth and goodness in our values—we are expanding our consciousness of reality and adding a new and deeper dimension to our thinking and actions—in effect we are beginning to transfer our "seat of identity" to a higher level of thinking and acting. When this happens those spirit realities start to be revealed as a part of the reality reflected in our very own experiences. It can also give us the ability to correct and balance our emotions because these realities are stabilising; they start to remove the selfish qualities of love and improve our conscience that acts as a guide and can influence the direction our material thinking takes.

The goodness of love is potentially directive. When we chose to make it our highest value and place it into our keystone, we become aware of an innate ability to enhance and unify our emerging concepts of truth, beauty, and goodness which in turn—because of their relationship to the basic elements—gives us a wholeness and a unified view of reality. The beauty of encompassing the goodness of love is that, through our personality, we can safely and simply start to function as one as we have been able to unify all the elements of reality! Our mind seems to be geared to function within emerging levels of understanding reality. Our personality is becoming more real in its growing relationship to this golden gift within us that comes from the first cause—this spirit-value nucleus of Love. And once more I think it's worth repeating this: …herein lies a great mystery; the more a person approaches reality through the goodness of love the greater the reality—the actuality—of that person.

By introducing this "kicker"—by deciding to place this love—this goodness of love—into our golden value keystone and lock it in its place to be our highest directive value, it would have a drawing power to bring together all our values and place them under its parental care. It would become a valid addition to our outlook and provide a solid foundation for creative thinking and acting.

CHAPTER 9

Where Does the Soul Fit into the Picture?

The word "soul" is widely used in the world. It is used in a variety of ways in every walk of life and in all cultures. Yet what does it mean? What is it actually referring to? Here are some definitions from the Oxford Dictionary:

> A person's inner character, containing their true thoughts and feelings; the spiritual and moral qualities of humans in general; the spiritual part of a person; believed to exist after death; strong and good human feeling; especially that gives a work of art its quality or enables somebody to recognize and enjoy that quality. [12]

Examples of Usages:

> "music that soothes your soul"; "the eyes are the windows to the soul"; "there was a feeling of restlessness deep in her soul"; "the dark side of the human soul"; "in my view, fine art feeds the mind and soul". [12]

That's all well and good, but we haven't exactly revealed any scientific explanation as to what the soul is, but like the words "mind" and "spirit" we get an inner feeling about what is meant.

By combining all the elements of reality and embracing them with a whole heart we create something completely new—a new and different point of view, a deeper perception of reality, a growing wisdom of experience emerging from the combination of human experience and the truth of spirt realities.

The wonderful thing about Truth, whether it be objective or subjective, is that it always has some meaning and value attached to it. If there is no real value to be found within a so-called truth, then it is simply not true. The rewarding thing about the discovery and comprehension of truth is in its application, and the greater the truth, the higher its value. It is by the finite ladder of the insights of truth within our minds that enables us to climb up from the temporal and basic material realties towards a more enduring spiritual reality. Our understanding of reality is represented and reflected by our acting personality. When we allow the reality of truth to drive our thinking, over time it naturally produces a new and growing element to our thinking, one that is not entirely material nor completely spiritual. This new growing element contributes to an evolving part of our being.

If higher urges emanate from a spirit force that indwells our mind, another idea beckons consideration. With our reasoned belief in the validity of our own experiences, coupled with a faith that is based on those beliefs, perhaps it is reasonable to have faith that something is growing within us as a result of the relationship between our freewill thinking and that divine spark—the core value of the goodness of love that we have placed in our keystone. This "something" that is growing within us would open the way to enable us to transfer over time our purely material seat of identity from its temporal material consciousness to a larger viewing framework of mind that includes personally identifying with the more real and enduring spiritual nucleus within. When we choose to connect to the very creator of all life, a conspiracy of benign circumstances within us naturally gives birth to something new—something with an endless potential for growth—something we call the **Soul**.

As mentioned in an earlier section, when you add two elements together you can create a substance that is entirely new and often unexpected, like the properties of water. What scientist would ever guess—or even believe—that when you add two atoms of hydrogen to one of oxygen, you'd get water! (You'd think that if you combined the explosive and flammable properties of hydrogen and oxygen you would end up with something very dangerous indeed.) So if we use this as an analogy, what happens when the will of an individual personality simply chooses to make a moral decision—the beginnings of a natural partnership with the first cause of creation? **You get the birth of a soul!** And as that personality goes through life continuing to work in willing partnership with its divine spark within, you get the *growth* of that soul—something that can even survive after death. Our soul is our ticket to survival and is solely dependent on our freewill choosing to follow the leadings of this divine pilot.

By choosing to share our inner life with the spiritual realities in our mind arena of choice, when we observe and taste their fruits, our soul can act as a natural sifter and sorter and become a valued motivational force in our freewill choosing. At a very early age when we first begin to make moral choices, we inaugurate the birth of our soul. We are not highly conscious of it as it starts out as an embryonic part of our being but, because of the components that make us what we are, our soul has the potential to grow and develop, and as it grows it naturally becomes an integral part of our being.

Our purely material consciousness is capable of growing towards becoming spirit-conscious by simply being willing to share the inner life with our spiritual nucleus. Our material mind is capable of functioning on a higher level where the goodness of love can be felt and recognised by us as we become more trusting and cooperative towards its leadings. Once we are aware that there also lies before us in our journey of life greater spirit realities that emanate from love that are also there to be discovered and utilised in our thinking just waiting to be found, that they are just as real and alluring as everything else. Those higher realities that emanate from this core of love are those with which we can freely choose and wed to our understanding that we already possess; an ongoing soul growth and awareness of faith in love as we evolve and progress towards a wholeness of understanding of the truth contained within finite reality.

These value-unifying spirit elements of Love may very well be the salt that sustains and maintains us in our forward struggle towards a unity of identity and individuality. If more and more individuals embrace these spirit realities, then our collective fruits of the spirit will add a beauty to our society and aid in protecting the direction of our civilisation's continued growth. We may become more like a big family, one that recognises that we are all in this together!

As we tread the lowly paths of earthly existence, spiritual realities have the ability to water and fertilise the soil of our experiences and contribute to our accumulation of wisdom and the growth of our personal lives. Spirit realities, when recognized by our minds, spark a flame of truth that sheds light on a greater purpose to the adventure of living; value-adding to our experiences as we apply their light of truth; they simply enhance our ability for creativity and goodness in the world.

CHAPTER 10

The Womb of Finite Reality and Our Birth

The newly awakened relationship of the soul to our spirit nucleus is a bit like the relationship between a wise and true loving parent with its growing child; a wise and loving parent who guides and nurtures its child while not interfering with the child's freewill yet equipping it with all the tools it will need to function safely in the world; a wise and loving parent whose one desire is to see its children eventually achieve their individual creative potentials and to possess well balanced characters.

This line of thinking reminds me of the powerfully symbolic artwork of Michael Anglo's famous painting, *The Creation of Adam* depicting man reaching up to God, and God reaching down to man. For me it is a wonderful work of art in which to contemplate this idea of reaching up to touch on the truth of the immortal indwelling spirit who represents the personality that lies at the centre of all that is real and is behind the creation of the material universe. The touching of the fingers could be the knowing of our childlike soul, the will of each individual reaching up to join in cooperation with the will of

God; a re-birth of relational understanding of life and the universe around us. For me it symbolises the very truth of the relationship between us and the immortal spirit nucleus of the universal Father within us. It is indeed breathtaking!

We are herd creatures, and we have a herd-instinct with a common community spirit. But we are so much more—we have personality. You are unique. There is not another you in the whole universe. So, if you don't play your part someone else will, but they will do it their way, not yours. Your personal relationship to the universe and to other individuals is valued because of your unique contribution. You have the ability of mind to freely choose, grow, create, contribute, and share with others; you are of value! Of course, we can continue on the basic level of existence by just using the material side of our thinking foundation and concern ourselves only with the material side of life and be quite content and satisfied with ourselves, and practice to the best of our abilities the "do unto others as you would have them do unto you" code of ethic, but we are creative personalities, and this creativity has a strong and robust freewill. Our material understanding already has so much potential contained in it, but these insights can be enhanced and deepened by the spirit reality of the simple realisation that a gift of the goodness of love—the "water of life"— resides within us, and we can place our understanding of this gift into our highest value-level of our keystone and light up our lives. Its value, over time has the relational power to replace the selfish qualities of love and helps us to safeguard ourselves because of its ability to pilot, underpin, and envelop us. By thirsting for this water, it gives the goodness of love the ability to infuse itself into our inner life; it gives integrity to our unifying personality and contributes to a balanced and healthy self-respect while at the same time setting us free to grow and to become even more real and to open up unforeseen potentials of creativity. We are left with a feeling of liberation when we discover and experience the existence of the beauty of Love. This simple truth really does set you free from material bonds and gives you a feeling that we are not hopelessly alone in the universe. You are loved and valued by the parental first cause of reality; you are guided and protected by the goodness of love as if you were the only person that existed, and this relationship is valued because it is unique; it is one of a kind.

"It is fatal to man's idealism when he is taught that all of his altruistic impulses are merely the development of his natural herd instincts. But he is ennobled and mightily energized when he learns that these higher urges of his soul emanate from the spiritual forces that indwell his mortal mind. It lifts man out of himself and beyond himself when he once fully realizes that there lives and strives within him something which is eternal and divine. And so it is that a living faith in the superhuman origin of our ideals validates our belief that we are the sons of God and makes real our altruistic convictions, the feelings of the brotherhood of man." [2]

As we live and grow in the womb of finite reality, this embryonic, quasi-material, spiritually-evolving emerging soul—this natural metamorphosis of our emerging identity is built into the evolution of the creation of our being. Universe evolution has designed us to be inwardly responsive and reactive to all of the elements of reality that I have been talking about. Once we experience and recognise the ultimate value of the goodness of love and choose to place it into our value keystone, this gift of Love becomes the unifying heart of our completed archway of thinking. We realise that through this spiritual DNA we are personally related to the first cause through this gift within us which we place into our living keystone because we recognise its worth and truth. We can then realise that the universe has not completely left us alone, we now have this wonderful compass within us, our antidote to uncertainty; that we are not orphans living in a heartless cold mechanistic universe that is simply made up of material elements and chemicals. We are a part of creation; because of our soul, we are creating and participating in the actualisation and realisation of the unfolding of finite reality. This is the re-birth of our understanding of our existence.

Over time, and by our own freewill efforts, we embark upon a personal spiritual journey, and somewhere down the track, through our evolving soul, we may start seeing eye to eye with our indwelling spiritual nucleus and eventually, through this evolutionary growth of the soul, our individual personality can shine forth the qualities of divinity and this spirit nucleus can find expression through our personality. This is a transformation from the potential to the actual through the process of experience and freewill choosing in time; a re-birth of a new personal growing child of this finite universe literally comes into being!

If there is an immortal spirit at the very centre of our being; one that gently attempts to nurture the real value of our experiential growth—although this is very personal stuff—we are, after all personalities—the laws of the universe seem to uphold and reflect our freewill choices regardless of the consequences both inside and outside of ourselves.

I suspect it is our evolving soul that will ultimately choose between truth and error. It will be this growing soul that will eventually identify between reality and fiction. But within all of my speculation in this regard there is one thing, regardless of my uncertainty, of which I am fully convinced, and that is the will of the creator in its personal attitude towards us is **just and fair**. It fully understands about our vulnerable circumstances. After all, if the highest creative value contains the absolute personal prerogatives of the goodness of love, it must also contain an abundance of the parental qualities of understanding, forgiveness, and mercy towards those creatures it created, and it would naturally do all in its power to assist us while leaving us with the vital prerogative of freewill.

We live in a mysterious universe where there is a lot we don't comprehend about ourselves and creation.

"God created time to keep it all from happening at once." – *Micky Newberry, songwriter, Nashville* [13]

CHAPTER 11

Religion and Society

Science will never have a quarrel with the goodness of values. It may question the existence of spirit realities and the presence of personality in the first cause of creation, because these are realities that are impossible to prove by the scientific method which can only analyse material reality. However, the examination of values such as love and goodness do not belong to the material realm, therefore cannot be scientifically analysed.

What if the religions of the world are just lagging behind in their forward thrust of evolution? They are trying their best with what they have collected from the past but, to varying degrees, they have now become a wheel that's become caught up within a wheel that is driven by the axle of their tradition-bound sacred texts that hold on to formulated creeds derived from those texts and guided by their established dogmas and theologies. I'm sure that a vast majority of religionists following these traditions are sincere in their faith and endeavours, but they are human, and as humans we can be simply afraid and overly cautious about getting things wrong or about being open to new ways of thinking. It's only natural to be cautious and uncertain when belief is bound by established doctrines.

The attraction of science (even though it too has its problems), is that it is willing to revise itself every time it discovers more truth in facts. It is keen to do this because its goal is to find and understand more about the material workings of the universe. So, science has a legitimate role to play in religion regarding the truth in factual things. The beauty of science is that it destroys superstition and ignorance in regard to the truth in material things. But let's be fair; just because of the imperfections, incompleteness, and resistance to change inherent in the institutions of the world's religions, let's not make the mistake of disregarding the positive contributions they have given to the world. So for the time being, if you are sceptical about the world's religions, try reading their historical scriptures with an eye searching for those things that are beautiful, true and good. There are timeless truths contained in the pages of these sacred texts—after all they haven't survived down through the ages and touched so many souls for no reason. If we consider them in an historical context of evolving ideas about the nature and character of God and the quest for discovering a deeper understanding of the true characteristics and motivations of the personality of the goodness of love, we may see that humanity has been able to solve a number of problems by embracing the lessons gleaned from the timeless stories with valuable insights contained within these texts. The spirit of Budda's quest to work it out is greater than Buddhism. The universal teachings of Jesus and how he lived his inspirational life are much greater than Christianity. As long as our minds are grounded in the realities of the real world, we can safely contemplate the unknown. By holding up the flame of desire for truth within our hearts and minds we can abandon the darkness of fear of the unknown; we can live with uncertainties and honest doubts and contemplate the mystery of all those things yet to be discovered.

CHAPTER II

"Science investigates; religion interprets. Science gives man knowledge, which is power; religion gives man wisdom, which is control. Science deals mainly with facts; religion deals mainly with values. The two are not rivals." *[Martin Luther King Jr.]* [15]

"The modern age will refuse to accept a religion which is inconsistent with facts and out of harmony with its highest conceptions of truth, beauty, and goodness." [2]

Fear may have been the very beginning of wisdom, but our evolving insight and growing wisdom dictates that a God of love does not harbor the human attributes of revenge, jealously, fear, sacrifice, and retribution. To offer stability and direction in a changing and complex world, the world's religions need to put more effort into highlighting and sharing their already discovered gems of insightful teachings; they need to bring forth and present the gems that are worthy and relevant for humanity today; ones that are devoid of fear and superstition; ones that don't conflict with the findings of modern-day science. Then once identified, they should build onto, and expand their understanding of these gems that contain the beauty of truth and goodness and the dominance and compelling power of Love. The job of today's religions is not over for "just as surely as the butterfly eventually emerges as the beautiful unfolding of its less attractive creature of metamorphic development" *[2]* the world's religions must continue to evolve and present clearer and attractive insights into the fruits of spiritual realities; into the revelations of peace, joy and goodwill contained within the beauty of truth and the goodness of values. Love is the property of the human race simply because it belongs to everyone and is in everyone—this love does not belong to just a club of gifted or chosen individuals! For all of us grounded in the world, these realities will always remain vital and stable additives that should be included in our individual thinking, especially in this complex world. Religion needs to continue to explore the creator's personal relationship with the individual and present a clearer picture of how we are all related to one another. The elements of relationships cause a metamorphosis. Humans can grow out of their animal tendencies, and we can emerge as new and enduring personalities when we willingly embrace the goodness of love.

Social Cohesion—a Collective Consciousness

What is going to spark and light up the direction of all the things, meanings, and values in our personal world? What can protect us from too much confusion, uncertainty, and depression? What will protect us from disrespectful, antagonistic, and thoughtless attitudes towards those who hold differences of opinion? What can change our not-so-good innate habits and turn them into better and more cohesive ones? What will broaden our narrow likes and dislikes and expand our interests that cause us to change our attitudes towards others? What will enlighten us to see the truths that may be contained in different viewpoints? What will safeguard us from harbouring revenge and hatred towards others? What could inspire us to eliminate the selfish qualities of love in our varied relationships? How does our society produce a safe, friendly, adventurous, and meaningful environment for youth to grow in? What will safeguard and promote a balanced self-respect of oneself, while at the same time giving us an understanding of the value, sanctity, and integrity of the individuality of each person? What will bind us together as brothers and sisters while at the same time prevent us from all having to think the same? What will promote peace and goodwill throughout humanity? These are critical questions we should reflect upon if we want to improve the quality of our societies and civilizations.

CHAPTER 11

A democracy works well when there is a common cohesiveness within society. If this cohesiveness breaks down, democracy, in and of itself, cannot provide it. Whether we all know it or not, spiritual realities are most important to individuals as they are vital elements that have contributed to our advancement at important junctions of our evolution and have provided a cohesion to society that would just not be there without their inclusion. In our individual and collective desires for happiness and pleasure, (including the accumulated ideals of civilisations) when we play them out without the spirit reality of the goodness of love being our main inner driving force, we inevitably reach a point where our attempts to maintain cohesion adversely affects the freedoms of individuals! All the foibles of human nature cannot be addressed and controlled by legislation alone. As our world becomes more complex, and as the freedoms of individuality increase, it will become way too hard to control without spiritual cohesion. We could easily end up throwing up our hands in the air and say, "I'm just going to live my life; there are no answers to all of this, so whatever, I'm not going to stress out thinking about it anymore." (And herein lies a big problem for social cohesion.) We can't change the course of history, but we can change the direction of future civilisation.

Not every rational idea or ideal that seems like a good idea turns out to be a good one in the long run. We are full of an abundance of creative imagination and ideas but if we think them through—play them out in our minds—we dump many of them because we can foresee that they would end up having undesired outcomes. Of course, many of our ideas have, and will continue to contribute to our laws and culture in positive ways, strengthening a foundation where we can participate, enjoy, and respect one another. But in a complex world where we have achieved so much and our material lives have become so much easier, a disease of narrow self-interest can creep in where there is little cohesion in our complex society and the future gradually becomes uncertain. In such a volatile environment we may come up with philosophies, trends of pleasure-seeking, and new ideas for inventing or rearranging our idea of freedom of expression for all. When such new ideas start to be enforced upon a society through legislation, we run the risk of inadvertently curtailing the creative powers of freedom of expression and inevitably having to "cancel our culture" to justify the intended outcome. A continuation of cancelling out one's cultural inheritance only gets replaced with the invention of another which may end up playing out to be worse than the one it is attempting to improve or replace.

When public opinion accepts and advocates that this so-called freedom of rights is progressive there emerges a natural tendency to insist that it must be accepted by everyone. When the majority accepts this false sense of freedom the mores eventually tend to sanction it by adopting a uniformity of thought which, in turn, runs the risk of setting the stage for the death of respecting genuine differences of opinion which is the very thing that underpins a healthy democracy. Once society loses its appetite for the pursuit of truth—when it no longer allows for healthy debate when there are differences of opinion—we are left with the fear of not being able to express our opinions in case we upset someone, or worse still, get disbanded from professions or ostracised. Our society can drift into becoming divided and fragmented into tribal-like ideologies. The lack of qualitative thinking in mainstream society creates a vacuum for self-centeredness and antagonistic assertiveness coupled with a tendency to wilfully destroy the reputation of others who hold differing views.

If "love is the desire to do good to others", what if our innocent youth grow up in an environment that is not interested or couldn't be bothered seeing or knowing the difference between lust and love; what if they fail to see that their freedoms go hand-in-hand with individual growth, understanding, and responsibility? What sane philosophy could improve human behaviour, while at the same time encourage individual creativity and good will among humans? What sane ideas and ideals can safely transform our natural tendances to move away from the incessant clamouring of self—the selfish quality of love?

> "Liberty without the associated and ever-increasing conquest of self is a figment of egoistic mortal imagination. ... License masquerading in the garments of liberty is the forerunner of abject bondage." [2]

Biology ensures that there are essential differences between the sexes wherein each has equal value to the evolution of any species—one is by no means greater than the other. The evolution of civilisation as we know it has literally emerged from the essential cooperation between men and women. Teamwork and cooperation instead of competition between the sexes are essential ingredients for our continued progression. Many institutions have emerged that have contributed to stable societies. The family unit, where there is cooperation between men and women, has always been at the basis of the evolving institution of the family. The narrative suggesting that man knowingly took away women's rights and, over time as civilisation slowly advanced, begrudgingly handed them back, is a false narrative. It is unfair, cruel, and unproductive for either of the sexes to thoughtlessly belittle one another because of their inherent differences.

When we study anthropology and go back down through the ages, we observe that the environment in which our primitive ancestors lived was violent and dangerous. In this volatile environment woman was at a distinct disadvantage not only because of her physique but also because of her vulnerabilities associated with childbearing and noble maternal instincts. For example, picture a scene where a hungry sabretooth tiger leaps out from the darkness into the space of a man and a woman sitting by the fire. The woman screams and protectively grabs her child while the man leaps up, grabs his spear, and kills the tiger. The man naturally did this, and the woman was grateful; it was in her favour and to her advantage. Sex attraction brought us together and our natural instincts forged the beginnings of cooperation between the sexes because they were of mutual benefit. Woman needed a safe and stable home to rear her children, and man found it to his advantage to be involved in homemaking and provide ample protection to maintain the comforts and security of what they established together.

The quality of cooperation between men and women in the cultural institution of family life faithfully reflects the quality of any civilisation—social progress. It's only in relatively recent times that many of our cultures have developed environments that are much less violent and dangerous than in earlier times. This has allowed women in some cultures to achieve their well-earned rights for equality. While men and women are of equal value, they are not exactly the same—rather they are supportive and complimentary to each other. Women have willingly contributed to the ongoing momentum of advancing civilisation. While the term "might is right" may have been relevant in certain situations in a dangerous and violent world, even in those situations woman still contributed by courageously playing her part; both sexes have contributed equally to making the world a much safer, just, and fairer place. The religious idea that man has a divine right to lord it over woman is utterly false and borders on the ridiculous; a man earns the trust and respect of a woman through his motivations and deeds—through his efforts and actions; likewise does a woman earn the trust and respect of the man through her deeds, actions, and motivations. Their complimentary natures and the combination of perspectives, when brought together through cooperation in their common goals produces a powerful and formidable team.

FINITE LADDERS

CHAPTER 11

Finding the Compass

Where I lived when I was young there were two streets that ran down the back of my house filled with immigrants who, after the devastation of the end of the Second World War, immigrated to Australia from Europe. Living in these streets were Greeks, Yugoslavs, and Italians. Even though most of them hardly spoke any English, they were not difficult to get to know; hand signals and gestures were all that was needed for a kid like me to hit up a friendship. I used to marvel at their backyards—they were so different from ours—they were full of wonderful arrays of lush vegetable gardens which included chook pens and often a pigeon loft. As a kid I was really impressed with the idea of having pet birds that were free to go out and fly around and always managed to find their way home.

It wasn't too long before I talked my dad into letting me have a pigeon loft in our own back yard. I befriended two people I knew who had pigeons. They were easy to spot as the pigeons would fly around above their houses. One guy down the road had many different types of birds. He was a fireman and was a huge guy, six foot six with bright red hair who, to me, looked just like a Viking. After four in the afternoon, when he finished his work shift, I would go round to his place to ask questions and look at his birds. We used to sit on the back steps of his house for hours just looking at his pigeons and talking about them. It must have looked a site to see this huge burly guy in his fireman's uniform with brass buttons and big boots sitting next to this little skinny kid in a pair of shorts with both of us staring at the birds, soaking in the afternoon winter sun, and enjoying the tranquillity of the birds in and around his loft. He gave me four birds—a pouter, a fantail, and two racers. The other guy I found lived at the other end of our neighbourhood. He was a retired policeman; he had over fifty racing pigeons and above his fireplace on the mantel piece were trophies that he'd won for racing his birds. He was in a national pigeon racing club, and they used to ship the birds over two thousand miles away for the races.

On the weekends my friend Titch and I used to pick out a bird each from my loft, put them in a cardboard box with a few breathing holes, then tear off down to the train station and jump on the next train to the end of the line which was about forty miles away at a place called Hurstbridge; it felt like the end of nowhere. There was nothing at Hurstbridge—just a wooden platform, a post office letter box, and the sound of birds in the surrounding trees growing along a dusty dirt road heading off to who knows where. As soon as we got there, we ran over to an open field opposite the little station and let the birds free; they flew up then around a couple of times then disappeared. Meanwhile, the train driver had to change the tracks by pulling on a large leaver so that when the train departed it was on the other side of the tracks to take us back. We had just enough time to free the birds and jump on the train before it left. On our arrival home we would run from the station to my house. The birds always beat us. There they were sitting on their perch inside the loft looking like they hadn't been anywhere at all. It was a wonder to me and a mystery how these pigeons had this innate ability to find their way back and always beat us home. It was like they had some kind of inbuilt compass that I couldn't fully understand; such a small little brain capable of doing such amazing things.

So, keeping in mind the analogy of an inner compass indwelling a simple homing pigeon, let's ask these questions again: Has our freewill been entirely left alone in the universe? Does it have no guidance, no compass within to chart its course? Are we simply orphans in a cold materialistic universe doomed to make the most of just one short life? Is there no God whose personality encompasses the endless relationship of the goodness of love? Is there no hope for everlasting growth or survival of our selves or for the survival of any meaningful relationships we've had with one another? If we can't work it out within ourselves, would we dare to ask outside of ourselves, with the attitude of a little child looking up into the night sky saying, "I can't fully understand the meaning of my life and my relationship to the universe all by myself. I need help in trying to work it out and to find answers to these compelling questions."

Here is some food for thought:

"Your religion is becoming real because it is emerging from the slavery of fear and the bondage of superstition. Your philosophy struggles for emancipation from dogma and tradition. Your science is engaged in the age-long contest between truth and error while it fights for deliverance from the bondage of abstraction, the slavery of mathematics, and the relative blindness of mechanistic materialism.

"Mortal man has a spirit nucleus. The mind is a personal-energy system existing around a divine spirit nucleus and functioning in a material environment. Such a living relationship of personal mind and spirit constitutes the universe potential of eternal personality. Real trouble, lasting disappointment, serious defeat, or inescapable death can come only after self-concepts presume fully to displace the governing power of the central spirit nucleus, thereby disrupting the cosmic scheme of personality identity." [2]

Simply put, this means our values should be guided by the realities of our understanding of our "spirit nucleus" which I have previously demonstrated as being one and the same as the "goodness of love". If we don't take into account this nucleus of spiritual reality within us—if we don't take into account, the placing of our understanding of this Love into our value keystone of existence—we inevitably view the creation of the universe and ourselves as being composed simply of mechanistic atoms of matter—nothing else. This can become disheartening, philosophically confusing, and more than that—it can stifle our idealism and creativity. When you play out in your mind our human contribution to the formation and organisation of our civilisations and philosophies of life without the involvement of this spirit reality within, it becomes harder and harder over time to maintain genuine cohesion within our societies.

A Lasting and Cohesive Nucleus for Humanity

Our societies need common values to maintain their cohesiveness. What we collectively hold as known values creates this cohesiveness. The depth of the actuality of goodness in these values faithfully reflects the quality and advancement of a society. Early in the evolution of social development such things as one's clan, tribe, patch of land, common language, local and national customs, skin colour, familiarity, and evolving religious beliefs and political ideals created a cohesiveness within each society which gave people an identity and a sense of belonging. Modern societies, having evolved from these basic tribal needs of having to stick together for survival purposes, are not much different, yet everything now is on a larger scale and has become far more complex. More than ever, cultures and societies must learn to tolerate each other and live together despite their cultural differences in order to maintain a safer world for all. As a result of rapid social changes caused by advancing science and postmodernist thinking, we are starting to move away from many of the very foundations that once held our clans, tribes, and different nations and confederations together. Modern societies have naturally evolved their unique cultural flavours which have contributed to the richness of civilisation but now, at this stage of our evolution where we have become much more conscious of our world and how it works, we need peace between nations for survival; we need to realise that the role of values held by each individual underpins and drives not just our individual lives but also the direction of society as a whole. What is needed is a **shared common value**—one that is highly personal but can support and underpin the forward movement of all cultures and civilisations to create a foundation for a better and more enduring civilisation.

How can we learn to understand the worth of others and realise that every individual is of intrinsic value? By embracing an inner value that can illuminate and transform the truth of our lives, we can learn to adopt the idea that a divine spark—an immortal spirit—indwells each one of us; we all possess this spiritual nucleus within. By internalising this very simple idea we could have amazing transformations in our thinking and repercussions in attitudes towards others and the world we live in. Mankind as a whole has never seriously tried this. When we realise that there is a divine fragment of God indwelling everyone regardless of race, nation or culture, we realise, when engaging face-to-face with each other, that we are dealing with an individual who is also indwelt by the sanctity of the "will of creation". There's God deep within every individual; they have this same spirit nucleus as we do; there is a spirit of the goodness of love indwelling them making it much easier to understand, tolerate, respect and love them. There is, so to speak, deep inside them a light of beauty, truth, and goodness straight in front of us looking out through the eyes of that person. "The material eyes are truly the windows of the spirit-born soul. The spirit is the architect, the mind is the builder, the body is the material building." "He who formed the ear shall he not hear", "he who formed the eye shall he not see". *[2]*

The realisation of this common understanding coming directly from within us would naturally lift the ethical and moral bar of respect we have for one another. Such a common understanding has the power to lift the standards of justness and fairness and can easily create a genuine "desire to do good to others." In all our relationships with people, we would treat them as equals and act accordingly.

When we realise that this indwelling spirit is the parental component of each of our souls, we realise we are all related—we are indeed brothers and sisters of this same spirit within us. If this idea was adopted throughout the world, we could begin to witness the spreading of a "benign virus of love" that could trigger genuine efforts resulting in having universal "peace on Earth and good will among men". What we all hold as the greatest value would cause a rebirth of the spirit within each individual that becomes a shared "property of the human race". **This ideal is the one and only ingredient that can provide the vital cohesion the whole world needs to become truly stable in order to maintain sustainable civilisations.** No other philosophy of living will ever achieve this! History is littered with the damage of counterfeit ideals of Utopia. One of the best things about a philosophy of life for those who embrace this spirit nucleus within, is that they can keep it to themselves while going about their natural lives. By living in accordance with this spirit, they will naturally shine forth the fruits of the spirit which become apparent to others by the lives they live. As we become aware of the value of others and see the fruits of their spirit nucleus, in time there will be a renaissance of spiritual awareness that will result in harmonious societies that can live and work safely together.

The world's problem is the individual's problem. The world is only as good or bad as the accumulation of the choices of each individual. Collectively those individual choices make up the nature of our families, communities, nations, continents, and the entire world. Our personalities are imbedded in the soil of an evolving finite universe. While our personalities don't change, everything else about us has the potential to grow and change. The non-material domain within us is where our freewill operates, and this domain of our mind is the gateway to our spiritual nucleus. We exist in the creation of our own reality, and we have to live with the reality of what we create. But we have within us the ability to correct ourselves, to change and to grow our thinking beyond the dust of temporal living. We can have an external relationship with the personality of the first cause; this is made possible because there is a fragment of the first cause inside us—the spiritual nucleus. The first cause is actually assisting us from within as we conduct ourselves in our external relationships with others.

"Man, in his spiritual domain, does have a free will. Mortal man is neither a helpless slave of the inflexible sovereignty of an all-powerful God nor the victim of the hopeless fatality of a mechanistic cosmic determinism. Man is most truly the architect of his own eternal destiny." [2]

"The mechanistic philosopher professes to reject the idea of a universal and sovereign will, the very sovereign will whose activity in the elaboration of universe laws he so deeply reverences. What unintended homage the mechanist pays the law-Creator when he conceives such laws to be self-acting and self-explanatory!

"It is a great blunder to humanize God, except in the concept of the indwelling [spirit] but even that is not so stupid as completely to mechanize the idea of the First Great Source and Centre." [2]

"Spirit is the basic personal reality in the universes, and personality is basic to all progressing experience with spiritual reality. Every phase of personality experience on every successive level of universe progression swarms with clues to the discovery of alluring personal realities. Man's true destiny consists in the creation of new and spirit goals and then in responding to the cosmic allurements of such supernal goals of nonmaterial value." [2]

Keeping all this in the back of our minds, let's remember that our human contribution to the relationship with our spirit nucleus will always be evolutionary and experiential. As we contend with the material, intellectual and spiritual aspects of our lives we must continue to re-evaluate the facts when science discovers more truths, discern deeper meanings as our philosophy becomes more sophisticated, and acknowledge the spirt presence as our insights into values expand through our sincere efforts to grow our souls as our relationship with the goodness of love grows. If we don't keep the three realities of matter, mind, and spirit in balance in our lives, we cannot shine forth a balanced personality. Remember, if a personality is not balanced and unified it is like that three-legged stool that has one of the legs shorter or longer than the others. Think of the three legs of the stool as being matter, mind, and spirit, and of the seat holding the stool together—unifying it—as our personality. Do we want to project a real version of ourselves or one that is out of balance and not unified, disjointed? We need to take all this into account, act upon it, and move forward in our ongoing adventure of pursuing truth.

CHAPTER 12

Renewing Our Keystone

By outlining an argument for the necessity of adding to the processes of human thinking we must be willing to search for and include the spirit-reality elements emanating from love, (i.e., beauty, truth, and goodness) each of us do this in our own way knowing these elements can be found through an attempt to understand the will of the first cause. And for those who may be agnostic, regardless of any honest doubts, I'm sure you would agree that the elements of love, in the sense I have been presenting, are worthy values to embrace and include into your thinking process. To bring this about is quite simple—all we need to do is to re-new our material value keystone by simply recognising and including the goodness of love and acknowledging that it is our highest value; it is the spiritual reality of Love. We need to place our highest understanding of these spiritual realities above our other values when and if they differ. In doing this we take another step onto a rung of the finite ladder; we have made the decision.

"Are your ideals sufficiently high to ensure your eternal salvation while your ideas are so practical as to render you a useful citizen to function on earth in association with your mortal fellows? ... Render to the Caesars the things which are material and to God those which are spiritual." [2]

When we experience the truth of this revelation, we need to recognise and understand that only within the actual spiritual nucleus—the guiding divine spark within us—are these realities of love (spiritual truth, beauty, and goodness) absolute, divine and eternal. On our human side there is a huge Grand-Canyon gap to eternal reality. We are partial, we are experiential and growing, and we understand the first cause from the perspective of finite understanding. Simply put, it's like having an endless well of water inside us from which we can draw as we grow in our personal experiences within finite reality. But it is through the knowing and feeling of this spiritual love that we can realise we are all connected; it is through this spiritual love that we recognise our personal relationship with the creator of the universe.

We achieve this through sincere efforts to share our inner lives with the first cause; it can start out as a faith relationship—a childlike moment of revelation; a confirmation that you are loved and not alone in the universe; a connection may happen in a crisis or it may slowly just dawn upon us; a connection may happen when we have a thoughtful and enlightened moment; it may happen when we look up and ask a bunch of sincere questions that we don't have answers to; it may happen when we ask for help in those important personal situations in our lives where we are unsure what to say or do; it may happen when we do some factual mediation when sorting out some problems in our life. For me it was simply walking out at night into the middle of a football field on a moonless clear winter's night, looking up to the stars and asking, "I really don't know, but I know there's got to be something to all of this; I really want to know, I'm not going away until I get some kind of answer." After coming back from standing in the middle of that football field, all I was left with was a feeling that I wasn't completely alone in the universe. It was then that I realised that personality was involved in it; this was when the universe came alive for me. It gave me a layer of meaning and appreciation that otherwise would just not have been there in my life if it were a purely material and mechanistic universe. Of course, I can't prove this experience but if anyone else has had a similar experience then, I suppose, they may relate to it.

It is from exactly here, our home, in the universe where we begin our adventure of understanding finite reality. Our mind, with its accumulated experiences, is the gateway to spiritual realities. Our universe has given us a challenge:

> "This is the true meaning of that divine command, 'Be you perfect, even as I am perfect,' which ever urges mortal man onward and beckons him inward in that long and fascinating struggle for the attainment of higher and higher levels of spiritual values and true universe meanings." [2]

Our human mind can understand the idea and ideal of this adventure and it can become loyal to the beauty, truth, and goodness that we find. And when it does, it naturally chooses this directive value-structure. It's there to be discovered—go and live your life to the full and don't let anyone stop you.

Positional Values

Let's examine value structures—how we position our values. As a lead in, below is a short exert from Dr. Jordan B. Peterson's book,

Beyond Order: 12 More Rules for Life. (Jordan Peterson is a clinical psychologist and professor of psychology.)

"…. it's necessary to consider the hierarchical manner in which we organize our value structures. We know that it is better to be a good person than a good parent or a good friend, as a good person subsumes good parent and good friend. It is better to be a good parent than to be a good cook, and better to be a good cook than a competent dicer and peeler of vegetables, for exactly the same reason. The ways in which we consider ourselves and others moral, in general—that is, properly oriented in the world; trustworthy; competent—are amalgams of micro-skills, sequenced into minor skills, arranged into expert abilities, compiled into higher-order values. You cannot teach a three-year-old child to clean his room by locking him in his room and commanding "clean your room." There is no reason to assume that he has the higher-order skills (and the corresponding moral value) that corresponds to that command: not without a lot of practice." [16]

Peterson points out "that it's better to be a good person than a good parent". What he has clearly identified is the top value of a value-structure for "good person" and "good parent or friend". He reminds us that when we are correctly orientated towards this value our positional value-structure grows according to our experience and maturity.

"Truth is coherent, beauty attractive, goodness stabilizing. And when these values of that which is real are co-ordinated in personality experience, the result is a high order of love conditioned by wisdom and qualified by loyalty. The real purpose of all universe education is to effect the better co-ordination of the isolated child of the worlds with the larger realities of his expanding experience. Reality is finite on the human level, infinite and eternal on the higher and divine levels." [2]

For us there is clearly an element of time involved in the blending of our human experiences with our perception of spirit realities. The beauty of these realities is that they add an endless growth-factor to our system of values. For creative personalities like us, we need to think deeply about the relationship between matter, mind, and spirit in our personal lives. Another way of expressing it would be the relationships between science, philosophy, and religion in the world. While they are all equally real, it is their positional arrangement that is important.

"Mind, matter, and spirit are equally real, but they are not of equal value to personality in the attainment of divinity. Spirit is the fundamental reality of the personality experience of all creatures because God is spirit. Spirit is unchanging, and therefore, in all personality relations, it transcends both mind and matter, which are experiential variables of progressive attainment." [2]

The quote below is a great little credo for our framework for thinking. You could spend hours unpacking and contemplating this quote, but the simple key to it, I believe, is the significance of systems in our thinking i.e., our "positional values".

"In aggregations parts are added; in systems parts are arranged. Systems are significant because of organization—positional values. In a good system all factors are in cosmic position. In a bad system something is either missing or displaced—deranged. In the human system it is the personality which unifies all activities and in turn imparts the qualities of identity and creativity." [2]

Spiritual realities may be the missing lens to enhance the ability of our minds to see and feel a stable and meaningful wholeness in the lives we live and to appreciate and enjoy the realness of creativity in the 'now', while at the same time being aware that our framework of reality is incomplete—it is an ongoing and growing process; **spirit realities give us the needed stability in our ever-changing world.**

The relationship of Love in the creation of reality is manifested by a personality! If we do not consider a first cause with personality, life would be just a relationship between our material selves and our environment, and we would take it all for granted. Why pause to contemplate the meaning and value of what's right here in front of us and be inspired by it to go on and consider the person behind its creation? Without pausing to do that it would be a bit like viewing an amazing painting hanging in the Louvre but the people walking past and pausing to linger over it—maybe even be seen to be moved by it and grasp some kind of value from it—are taking no interest at all in the artist and what motivated him or her. They are not moved to contemplate the reason why the artist created the darn thing in the first place! When our focus is always on ourselves, our material thinking framework focuses the value-aspect of our thinking on the benefit of self. When you look upon the creation of the universe without personality it can be viewed as a cold, cruel, meaningless, and empty space. By acknowledging that there's the possibility of a relationship with a loving and benign personality at the very centre of everything fundamentally changes our universal outlook.

> "All truth—material, philosophic, or spiritual—is both beautiful and good...... Health, sanity, and happiness are integrations of truth, beauty, and goodness as they are blended in human experience. Such levels of efficient living come about

CHAPTER 12

through the unification of energy systems, idea systems, and spirit systems." [2]

When we look at all of the possible components that go towards our thinking processes and unpack them—lay them all out and try and work out how each one contributes exactly to the working of our minds—we realise that it is incredibly complex; it could be likened to disassembling a car and laying out all the parts that go towards making it work—it looks like a complicated puzzle but when all the parts are put back together it simply functions as a single unit. You just stick in the key, turn it on and off you go.

"Life is really simple, but we insist on making it complicated."
– *Confucius* [4]

I have been trying to establish and identify that the importance of carefully positioning our values is key to a purposeful and meaningful life because it's our values that cause us to make our significant decisions! By eliminating the *selfish* qualities of love in the realms of our higher thinking, and gradually replace them with the *selfless* qualities of love coupled with the love of beauty, truth, and goodness, we gain the freedom to view everything differently; by identifying ourselves with the highest value of Love, we transfer our seat of identity and are driven by this heightened value. We're creating a higher reality within us; one that is neither entirely material nor self-centred. If this sounds a little complex, remember we are looking at all the components that contribute to our thinking processes. In reality our personalities pull it all together very nicely so we can function simply as one, as we are. Always remember that it's mainly our motives that drive us and it's what we value that determines our intent. It's quite simple; just place this highest value—the goodness of love—into the "golden value keystone" of your thinking.

Our minds work well when we can visualise concepts, ideas, and ideals through the use of symbolism that represents meanings and values because our minds readily relate to symbols. Creative thinkers like artists, architects, and designers generally use symbols to portray some kind of meaning in their works. It is easy to remember and visualise great truths by symbolising them. I came across a short sentence once that impressed me where the symbol of a ship was used to describe our mind. It inspired me to elaborate on this idea in order to present you with an analogy using the same symbolism that I hope will be helpful.

> "As we chart our course through finite reality, visualise our mind as a ship hoisting its billowing sales of things, meanings, and values while our personal freewill has its hand on the rudder of our emerging elements of truth, beauty, and goodness. The pilot of our vessel is our spirit nucleus, a universal gift—the will behind creation. It is this goodness of love within us which helps to guide us through and away from the jagged rocks and mudflats of our human foibles."

The ability for us to transcend ourselves is clearly the one thing that distinguishes us from the animal kingdom but because of this we will always be in that troublesome predicament of knowing less than we can believe. We have a two-fold relationship with the cosmos; on one hand we are a part of nature—we exist in and are bound by nature—on the other hand, we have the ability to transcend this nature. This causes our lives, from time to time, to be fraught with a little anxiety and uncertainty. In living our human lives, we are beset and challenged by many things in this human paradox. Here are some quotes that I'd like to share with you that highlight some of the problems we may face:

CHAPTER 12

"The courage required to effect the conquest of nature and to transcend one's self is a courage that might succumb to the temptations of self-pride. The mortal who can transcend self might yield to the temptation to deify his own self-consciousness. The mortal dilemma consists in the double fact that man is in bondage to nature while at the same time he possesses a unique liberty — freedom of spiritual choice and action. On material levels man finds himself subservient to nature, while on spiritual levels he is triumphant over nature and over all things temporal and finite. Such a paradox is inseparable from temptation, potential evil, decisional errors, and when self becomes proud and arrogant, sin may evolve." [2]

"The expansion of material knowledge permits a greater intellectual appreciation of the meanings of ideas and the values of ideals. A human being can find truth in his inner experience, but he needs a clear knowledge of facts to apply his personal discovery of truth to the ruthlessly practical demands of everyday life." [2]

"To the unbelieving materialist, man is simply an evolutionary accident. His hopes of survival are strung on a figment of mortal imagination; his fears, loves, longings, and beliefs are but the reaction of the incidental juxtaposition of certain lifeless atoms of matter. No display of energy nor expression of trust can carry him beyond the grave. The devotional labors and inspirational genius of the best of men are doomed to be extinguished by death, the long and lonely night of eternal oblivion and soul extinction. Nameless despair is man's only reward for living and toiling under the temporal sun of mortal existence. Each day of life slowly and surely tightens the grasp of a pitiless doom which a hostile and relentless universe of matter has decreed shall be the crowning insult to everything in human desire, which is beautiful, noble, lofty, and good. But such is not man's end and eternal destiny;

such a vision is but the cry of despair uttered by some wandering soul who has become lost in spiritual darkness, and who bravely struggles on in the face of the mechanistic sophistries of a material philosophy, blinded by the confusion and distortion of a complex learning. And all this doom of darkness and all this destiny of despair are forever dispelled by one brave stretch of faith on the part of the most humble and unlearned of God's children on earth." [2]

"Some men's lives are too great and noble to descend to the low level of being merely successful. The animal must adapt itself to the environment, but the religious man transcends his environment and, in this way, escapes the limitations of the present material world through this insight of divine love. This concept of love generates in the soul of man that superanimal effort to find truth, beauty, and goodness; and when he does find them, he is glorified in their embrace; he is consumed with the desire to live them, to do righteousness." [2]

"This saving faith has its birth in the human heart when the moral consciousness of man realizes that human values may be translated in mortal experience from the material to the spiritual, from the human to the divine, from time to eternity." [2]

"Paradise values of eternity and infinity, of truth, beauty, and goodness, are concealed within the facts of the phenomena of the universes of time and space. But it requires the eye of faith in a spirit-born mortal to detect and discern these spiritual values." [2]

Faith in the goodness of love is not a fanciful illusion as was revealed to me in my relationship and conversation with my father-in-law that I previously shared. Observation of the material aspects of the universe shows us that the universe is very efficient; everything gets re-cycled and renewed, nothing at all seems to be wasted. And I suspect it is the same in the realms of accumulated values of personal experience; everything of real value is also somehow salvaged. It is never wasted in this great universal enterprise.

Image: Freepik.com

CONCLUSION

As we get caught up in the business of day-to-day life it is easy to put off, or ignore, or simply forget to take an interest in even the basic maintenance of our physical health or more importantly our contemplation of the meaning of our lives. We naturally develop and inherit habit patterns, but we also have the ability to create, maintain, or even change our habit patterns for better ones; this is an important and ongoing challenge for us all. It is our focus and the decisions we make that determine what kind of goals we set in our efforts to improve and understand our lives. Whether it be our physical health, maintaining relationships, recreational gratification, or reversion, all these things put together balance the toil and grind of our day-to-day living by giving us renewed energy and a sense of direction, purpose, and satisfaction. We know there is no sense of achievement and advancement in living without intelligent effort. We also know that many of these worthy efforts do not always produce lasting joy or give us a permanent peace of mind.

So to summarise my understanding of the inner workings of our minds; on one side we have the basic elements that relate to our material and rational approach in our relationship to the universe, and on the other we have the emerging elements that lead us to an endless discovery of realities that are derived from our higher-minded personal relationship to the first cause. In the main, the basic elements are enough for us to develop reason and understanding in relation to the facts of science in our day-to-day lives and the evolvement of our experiences with the values of ethics and morality. These are necessary components that provide the foundation, or the soil, that is needed for our growing awareness of the essential emerging values of beauty, truth, and goodness that lead us to the heights of embracing the goodness of love and placing it in our golden value keystone.

When we view life from the basic levels of mind, we understand that our minds have an innate ability to operate with the basic elemental trilogy. This is how we work with, perceive, and discover finite reality. Then overlaying this basic reality is our emerging reality of values, continuing upwards to the highest value of all which sits at the very centre of our golden keystone. Now view it from the top downwards: we have the flowing repercussional effects of the goodness of love which reaches down and corrects, enriches, and enhances our evolving concepts of truth, beauty and goodness, which in turn reach down to influence the way we use our inherent qualities for responding to things, meanings and values. The lower levels of reality flow in at the bottom and the higher levels of reality flow down from the top giving us a sweet blending of the two; a growing understanding and viewpoint of the wholeness of our finite reality.

There seems to be plenty of room in our minds to accommodate a rich blend of all these components. There's a well within us that is bottomless and it is there for us to draw the refreshing life-giving water needed for our ongoing journey. We can be sensitive and openly willing to allow the spirit of truth to guide us in our daily arena of choice. We can have the best of both worlds in our thinking system—material/tangible and spiritual/intangible—that can create in us a quality that's unique; a quality that is not material yet not quite spiritual; a quality that is growing and gives in us a new more permanent and stable value of ourselves—i.e., the evolving immortal soul.

CONCLUSION

When I look into and realise how big and mysterious the universe is, I often ponder that in this world's playground of life, we are just on the first rung of the monkey bar of experience; we go from here to over there, and then over there to somewhere else. Keep a strong grip on the growing personal values of your life. Live this life to the full; adopt the purposeful aspiration in your heart and mind that this life is just the beginning of an unending adventure of discovery. Never underestimate the all-powerful value of the goodness of love. It is the creative force that sustains and drives the mechanisms of the universe.

So, in those quiet times when you have the pleasure to enjoy your own company, when you are completely alone with the universe, put aside a little time for the contemplation of the meaning of life. Give some thought to your position and relationship to the universe and give some gratitude to the person behind its cause; it is here where you can intimately share your inner life and your sincere questions with someone who fully understands you.

"Faith most willingly carries reason along as far as reason can go and then goes on with wisdom to the full philosophic limit; and then it dares to launch out upon the limitless and never-ending universe journey in the sole company of TRUTH." [2]

THE END

REFERENCES

I have simplified the References for the quotes used throughout this book. Each quote has a number at the end. Simply take note of this number and look up the corresponding number within this list of references below.

At the end of this list of I have included some selected quotes from two great thinkers: Albert Einstein and Confucius.

[1] Albert Einstein — Born March 14, 1879, Ulm, Württemberg, Germany—died April 18, 1955, Princeton, New Jersey, U.S., German-born physicist who developed the special and general theories of relativity and won the Nobel Prize for Physics in 1921 for his explanation of the photoelectric effect. Einstein is generally considered the most influential physicist of the 20th century.
https://www.goodreads.com/author/quotes/9810.Albert_Einstein

[2] The Urantia Book — First published in 1955 by Urantia Foundation, 533 W. Diversey Pkwy. Chicago, IL 60614 USA.
https://www.urantia.org

[3] Difference Between Mind and Brain — Research Gate
Post by: Devraj Wodeyar
https://www.researchgate.net/post/What_is_difference_between_mind_and_brain

REFERENCES

[4] Confucius — Born: 551 B.C., died: 479 B.C. at age 72. Place of Birth: The State of Lu, present day Shantung China, married at age 19, served as a government official for the State of Lu, eventually rising to the rank of Minister. He had a falling out with the ruler and then embarked on his career as a wandering sage and philosopher. Confucius's teachings emphasized benevolence (jen), reciprocity (shu), respect and personal improvement. His teachings were the foundation of Confucianism, which became China's state religion until the Communist Revolution. Confucius viewed himself as a transmitter who invented nothing. His teachings emphasized the importance of study and education. His goal was not a systematic theory of life or a society that was based on formal tradition. The goal of his philosophy was to have people think for themselves, and to improve themselves by emulating exemplars of moral righteousness. "Without thought for far off things, there shall be trouble near at hand."

[5] What is the Scientific Method? — Excerpt from Encyclopaedia Britannica
https://www.britannica.com/science/scientific-method

[6] What Do Postmodernists Believe? — Brian Duignan
https://www.britannica.com/topic/postmodernism-philosophy

[7] Definitions of Aspects of Postmodernism — Wikipedia
https://en.wikipedia.org/wiki/Postmodern_philosophy

[8] The Bible, Luke 10:25-37 — The Good Samaritan, (King James Version)

[9] Biblical quotes from Jesus reinstated in *The Urantia Book* — Note: While the wording is not exactly the same as the words in the King James Bible the meaning is very much the same. Here's the comparison between the two books:

The Urantia Book:
"... You are not to go hence in the proclamation of the kingdom, saying, 'it is here' or 'it is there,' for this kingdom of which you preach is God within you."

"...Seek first the kingdom of God, and when you have found entrance thereto, all things needful shall be added to you."

"...The faith of Jesus visualized all spirit values as being found in the kingdom of God; therefore he said, "Seek first the kingdom of heaven.""

King James Bible:
"Neither shall they say, lo here! or, lo there! for, behold, the kingdom of God is within you." Luke 17:21 KJV

"But seek ye first the kingdom of God, and his righteousness; and all these things shall be added unto you." Matthew 6:33 KJV

"But rather seek ye the kingdom of God; and all these things shall be added unto you. "Luke 12:31 KJV

"Jesus answered, 'my kingdom is not of this world'" John 18:36 KJV

[10] Excerpts from published articles — University of Columbia 2012

[11] RAF WW2 Fighter Pilots, Squadron 64 — Johnny Plagis & Francis Swadling
https://acesofww2.com/rhodesia/aces/plagis/
https://en.wikipedia.org › wiki › John_Plagis

[12] *Definition of the Soul* — Excerpts from *The Oxford Dictionary*

[13] Micky Newberry—Nashville Songwriter
https://www.mickeynewbury.com/biomain.htm

REFERENCES

[14] Martin Luther King Jr.
Born: 15 January 1929, Atlanta, GA, USA, died: 4 April 1968, Memphis, TN, USA. Martin Luther King dreamt that all inhabitants of the United States would be judged by their personal qualities and not by the colour of their skin. In April 1968 he was assassinated by a white racist. Four years earlier, he had received the Nobel Peace Prize for his nonviolent campaign against racism.
https://www.nobelprize.org/prizes/peace/1964/king/biographical/

[15] Dr. Jordan Peterson – (born 12 June 1962) is a Canadian Clinical Psychologist, YouTube personality, author, and a professor emeritus at the University of Toronto.
https://www.jordanbpeterson.com

Books by Peterson:

(1999) Maps of Meaning: The Architecture of Belief. Routledge. ISBN 978-0-415-92222-7.

(2018) 12 Rules for Life: An Antidote to Chaos. Penguin Random House. ISBN 978-0-345-81602-3.

(2021) Beyond Order: 12 More Rules for Life. Penguin Random House. ISBN 978-0-735-27833-2.

Albert Einstein — Selected quotes:

"The world as we have created it is a process of our thinking. It cannot be changed without changing our thinking."

"I am enough of an artist to draw freely upon my imagination. Imagination is more important than knowledge. Knowledge is limited. Imagination encircles the world."

"If you can't explain it to a six year old, you don't understand it yourself."

"If you want your children to be intelligent, read them fairy tales. If you want them to be more intelligent, read them more fairy tales."

"Logic will get you from A to Z; imagination will get you everywhere."

"Life is like riding a bicycle. To keep your balance, you must keep moving."

"Anyone who has never made a mistake has never tried anything new."

"A clever person solves a problem. A wise person avoids it."

"Science without religion is lame, religion without science is blind."

"Any fool can know. The point is to understand."

"If we knew what it was we were doing, it would not be called research, would it?"

"I have no special talents. I am only passionately curious."

"Try not to become a man of success. Rather become a man of value."

"The important thing is not to stop questioning. Curiosity has its own reason for existence. One cannot help but be in awe when he contemplates the mysteries of eternity, of life, of the marvellous structure of reality. It is enough if one tries merely to comprehend a little of this mystery each day."

"I know not with what weapons World War III will be fought, but World War IV will be fought with sticks and stones."

"You never fail until you stop trying."

"Great spirits have always encountered violent opposition from mediocre minds."

"The measure of intelligence is the ability to change."

"Gravitation is not responsible for people falling in love."

"It is not that I'm so smart. But I stay with the questions much longer."

Confucius — Selected quotes:
https://www.thoughtco.com/best-confucius-quotes-2833291

"It does not matter how slowly you go so long as you do not stop."

"When anger rises, think of the consequences."

"When it is obvious that the goals cannot be reached, don't adjust the goals; adjust the action steps."

"Faced with what is right, to leave it undone shows a lack of courage."

"To be able under all circumstances to practice five things constitutes perfect virtue; these five things are gravity, generosity of soul, sincerity, earnestness, and kindness."

"To see what is right, and not to do it, is want of courage or of principle."

"Before you embark on a journey of revenge, dig two graves."

"Success depends upon previous preparation, and without such preparation, there is sure to be failure."

"Do not impose on others what you yourself do not desire."

"Men's natures are alike, it is their habits that carry them far apart."

"Our greatest glory is not in never falling, but in rising every time we fall."

"Real knowledge is to know the extent of one's ignorance."

"Hold faithfulness and sincerity as first principles."

"The will to win, the desire to succeed, the urge to reach your full potential... these are the keys that will unlock the door to personal excellence."

"Study the past if you would define the future."

"Wheresoever you go, go with all your heart."

"Wisdom, compassion, and courage are the three universally recognized moral qualities of men."

"Forget injuries, never forget kindnesses."

"Life is really simple, but we insist on making it complicated."

"The more man meditates upon good thoughts, the better will be his world and the world at large."

"The superior man understands what is right; the inferior man understands what will sell."

"He who will not economize will have to agonize."

"If I am walking with two other men, each of them will serve as my teacher. I will pick out the good points of the one and imitate them, and the bad points of the other and correct them in myself."

"Ignorance is the night of the mind, but a night without moon and star."

"It is easy to hate and it is difficult to love. This is how the whole scheme of things works. All good things are difficult to achieve, and bad things are very easy to get."

"Without feelings of respect, what is there to distinguish men from beasts?"

www.ingramcontent.com/pod-product-compliance
Lightning Source LLC
Chambersburg PA
CBHW011801090426
42811CB00007B/1008